RUSS ALAN
PRINCE

HANNAH SHAW
GROVE

RICHARD J.
FLYNN

Fame &
Fortune

MAXIMIZING CELEBRITY WEALTH

To Jerry, a superstar

– *Russ*

For more than a decade, to DEC

– *Hannah*

To my family, especially
Gayle, Hilary, Ryan and Logan –
thanks for making my journey so
rewarding and enjoyable, and for
continuing to provide your love,
motivation and support.

– *Rick*

Table of Contents

Foreword

At Elite Traveler, it's our business to understand the luxury consumer and the products and services they care most about. Since its launch in 2001, *Elite Traveler* has been an integral part of the luxury lifestyle and an indispensable resource for those who want to surround themselves with the finest of everything.

We have long relied on the unparalleled research of Prince & Associates, Inc. to help us learn more about the preferences and behaviors of wealthy and powerful individuals. As part of our commitment to the high-end market, we regularly work with Prince & Associates, Inc. to conduct surveys on vacation and holiday luxury spending, the effect of geopolitical events on private jet travel, the effect of environmental factors such as market volatility and election results on spending, purchasing intentions in specific luxury retail sectors, and other topical subjects. These projects, along with some exciting new endeavors, underscore our intention to be the most informed partner for luxury consumers and purveyors, and the must-read magazine for new jet setters worldwide.

I was intrigued when Russ and Hannah suggested that *Elite Traveler* start a book publishing division to specialize in the ultra-high-net-worth. Our inaugural publication, *Fame & Fortune*, is a natural fit with our overarching editorial mission and helps shed light on an important constituent of the wealthy population: celebrities. In this book, Russ and Hannah have delivered their typically superior research-based insights coupled with valuable lessons from their hands-on experience working with exceptionally affluent families.

Fame & Fortune should be mandatory reading not only for celebrities with wealth to protect and enhance, their business managers, attorneys, and other advisors – but anyone curious about the intersection of money and notoriety will find this book to be both entertaining and illuminating.

DOUGLAS D. GOLLAN
President and Editor-in-Chief
Elite Traveler, the private jet lifestyle magazine

About this Book

We three authors – in our early careers and in our current work together – have focused on helping affluent individuals, like you, preserve and enhance their wealth. Over time, we have refined the processes and systems that have been most effective for our affluent clients and established our reputations as experts and specialists in this small, but extremely powerful, universe through extensive case experience and research, publishing, and lecturing on the topic.

Over time we have learned that wealthy individuals respond best when their unique qualities and preferences are acknowledged and incorporated into their service experience. As a result, we rely heavily on segmentation analysis to help us identify discrete groups of wealthy people that share certain demographics and behavior. The combination of our hands-on experience and our empirical research provides evidence that affluent celebrities are one of these segments. The facts surrounding their profession, lifestyle, wealth, relationships, and priorities are so distinct – and markedly different from most other high-net-worth individuals – that they warrant special attention.

The more we worked with celebrities, the more we tailored our personal and business approaches accordingly. Eventually these clients, and more often than not the advisors in their inner circle, asked for a primer on wealth preservation and enhancement – not to take matters into their own hands, but to engage more effectively in the process.

There are a number of holistic solutions for celebrity wealth that should be considered, but to provide sufficient attention to a very intricate subject, we chose to focus solely on advanced planning strategies in this book. These are the legitimate and proven ways to maintain, protect, and increase your net worth and they rely on our ability to navigate the tax code, maneuver through changing legal and regulatory environments, and capitalize on nuances in laws. Once goals are set and opportunities are identified, they are realized through sophisticated legal structures and select financial products.

The aspects of advanced planning we will address in *Fame & Fortune* will help you:

> Keep as much of your wealth as possible by securing it from litigants, creditors, and random opportunists;

> Plan for the most tax-wise, posthumous distribution of your wealth to the people and charities you choose; and

> More effectively manage and minimize your range of current tax obligations.

The bottom line is that effective advanced planning can help you stay wealthy – and become even wealthier.

WHAT YOU CAN EXPECT

Based on feedback from our celebrity clients and their other advisors, we wanted this book to accomplish the following objectives:

> Construct a research-based view of the world of a celebrity – we wanted to understand the aspects of a wealthy celebrity's life that can impact his or her finances, decision-making, and interactions with service providers.

> Introduce the advanced planning process – given its relatively low profile, we wanted to explain the philosophy and strategy behind advanced planning and how it relates to other parts of the financial and legal planning process.

Exemplify some key wealth enhancement, estate planning, and asset protection strategies – one of the easiest ways to bring an idea to life is through the use of examples, so we briefly present nine blind case studies of actual advanced planning solutions for celebrity clients.

Provide guidance on finding, choosing, and working with an advanced planner – years of experience coupled with extensive empirical research has given us insights into the essential qualities of a superior advanced planning experience, which we present as guidelines for you and your advisors to use as you navigate the process.

Reinforce the importance of expertise and legality – advanced planning is a highly specialized discipline that requires the technical proficiency and experience of an expert who operates within the letter of the law, as anything less can have disastrous results.

Our sincere hope is that the book you hold in your hands will help you prioritize your financial goals, make more informed decisions about your assets, pursue the strategies that can perpetuate and grow your net worth, and allow you and your loved ones to benefit from, and enjoy, your wealth to the greatest extent possible.

| I |

Spotlight on
CELEBRITIES

1

THE LENS OF
Celebrity Wealth

**AT A
GLANCE**

Celebrities are a breed apart and face different challenges than other wealthy individuals.

While they are largely male, which is consistent with most wealthy populations, celebrities are much younger than most individuals with comparable levels of wealth and therefore have longer to live and more time to earn and manage their money.

Based on the way they perceive themselves and their careers, celebrities fall into two psychographic segments – those that are status-oriented and those that are craft-oriented.

Celebrities who are status-oriented are more likely to be wealthier, consider themselves a business, feel stressed out by the demands of their career, and have a more intense fear of failure.

By contrast, celebrities that are craft-oriented tend to have less overall wealth and be less focused on the business aspects of their career. They are also more aware of the fleeting nature of celebrity.

Wealthy individuals

have been our clients for many years. We work with them, for them, and alongside them to identify opportunities and solve problems. We use empirical research to better understand their behavior, preferences and perspectives, and then use that information to create more sophisticated solutions, have more effective planning and working sessions, and help them or their advisors make more informed business decisions. One of the things we have learned is that the source of an individual's wealth is one of the most influential factors in a person's life. It colors their view of the world, their willingness to take risk, and their highest priorities and concerns, among other things.

The majority of today's private wealth has been generated by, and is still under the control of, business people. In fact, a fairly small percentage of the significant wealth in the world is from entertainment-related sources. It is, however, the most visible form of wealth and that makes it very different. While so many affluent individuals choose to live their lives out of the spotlight and establish support structures that shield them from unwanted attention, this is not possible – or even desirable – for many high-profile individuals. There is a nearly insatiable interest in how celebrities spend their time and money and, as a result, there are a number of media outlets dedicated to the subject. This scrutiny alone adds a facet to the wealth that does not exist for many other affluent people. In addition, celebrities often attract a disparate group of people all looking for something – employment, connections, friendship, endorsement-by-association, introductions, opportunities, a piece of the action – and this is another unusual factor that must be considered. And finally, celebrity wealth is often fleeting compared to many other sources of wealth – capable of providing windfalls in short periods of time that can quickly dry up when circumstances change. These reasons alone are enough to distinguish celebrities with wealth from the rest of the affluent universe. But fame can have far-reaching effects, and we found that celebrities are unique in other ways that can impact their financial objectives.

Delivering exceptional, highly effective financial solutions to complicated financial challenges is dependent on having a comprehensive understanding of a client's mindset, resources, desires, and limitations. For this book, we conducted an extensive research study to truly understand the core issues of celebrity wealth, starting with the basics:

| How big are their fortunes and how did they make their money?

| How old are today's rich celebrities and how much do they influence the direction of their careers?

| Are they happy?

| What are the greatest joys of their profession?

| What are the downsides to fame?

| To whom do they turn for financial guidance and what keeps them up at night?

Then we moved on to thornier issues – ones that many celebrities have not yet addressed.

> How prepared are they for an unexpected lawsuit or a nasty divorce?

> Could they be paying less in taxes?

> What if they're the victim of a kidnapping or identity theft?

> If something happens to them, will their estates be distributed in the way they want them to be?

Collectively, these insights can function as a blueprint for the rest of the celebrity world, while helping us establish a benchmark for needs and a way to prioritize issues.

To reach celebrities with considerable and verifiable wealth, we turned to entertainment attorneys. These professionals have long-standing relationships with their clients and a relatively intricate knowledge of their financial, business and personal affairs. We relied on an accepted social sciences research methodology called intermediary-based judgment sampling, a process in which a go-between is used to gather information from a hard-to-reach population. During the first-half of 2007 we worked closely with 203 such attorneys to gather information on five of their celebrity clients. In some cases the attorneys spoke with their clients to collect the requested data, and in others the attorneys responded on behalf of their clients based on their empirical and experiential knowledge of them. In all cases, the celebrities studied met all the following criteria:

> They were at least 25-years old;

> They had a net worth of at least US$10 million;

> They had a business association of five years or more with their entertainment attorney; and

> They had a close personal relationship with their entertainment attorney.

Our study – the first empirically valid analysis of celebrities available to the public – includes results on a total of 1,015 celebrities from around the world with an average net worth of US$37 million and a median net worth of US$25 million. More than half the subjects were actors, almost 40 percent were musicians and 5 percent were models (Exhibit 1.1). It's important to note that these were identified as the primary professions, however many of the celebrities may also work in another field that provides them with meaningful income – for instance, a supermodel acting in films or a recording artist designing her own line of apparel – and for some, a portion of their overall net worth is from investments and ventures outside the entertainment business. We specifically excluded professional athletes from this survey; while they certainly have celebrity status, the unique aspects of athletes and their wealth are so numerous they require a dedicated study.

EXHIBIT 1.1: *Primary Claim to Fame*

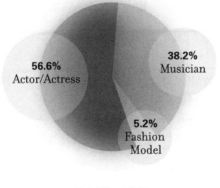

56.6%
Actor/Actress

38.2%
Musician

5.2%
Fashion
Model

N=1,015 celebrities
(based on 203 entertainment attorneys)

Within the group of 1,1015 celebrities, we identified two distinct segments using a cluster analytic segmentation methodology based on their orientation toward their professions (Exhibit 1.2). Slightly more than two-thirds of the celebrity sample was comprised of individuals strongly focused on the status associated with their careers. These types of professionals understand that a high-profile can translate into preferential treatment, new opportunities and favorable contracts, and the right reputation can confer power and status. By contrast, the remainder of the celebrities in the study were strongly focused on mastering the craft of their chosen field. These types of professionals are more interested in skill development and high-quality professional opportunities that match their interests and strengths.

EXHIBIT 1.2: *Orientation*

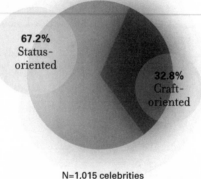

67.2%
Status-
oriented

32.8%
Craft-
oriented

N=1,015 celebrities
(based on 203 entertainment attorneys)

These segments help illustrate a philosophical and psychological difference in how celebrities approach and work in their professions and, as we'll discuss in the following section, they also play a major role in wealth creation and the way career success, failure and longevity are perceived.

PERSPECTIVES ON WEALTH

When viewing wealth by segment, those celebrities that were status-oriented had amassed larger fortunes than craft-oriented individuals. Status-oriented celebrities had an average net worth of US$42 million and a median net worth of US$30 million. Craft-oriented celebrities had an average net worth of US$26 million and a median net worth of US$16 million. These lower asset levels may indicate a willingness to pass on high-paying jobs in favor of those that resonate more strongly with their personal ethos (Exhibit 1.3).

EXHIBIT 1.3: *Wealth by Orientation*

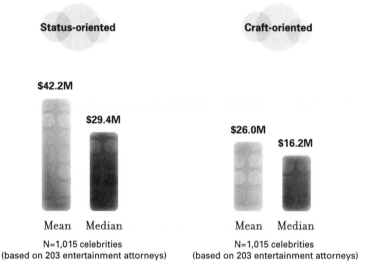

Status-oriented   **Craft-oriented**

Mean	Median	Mean	Median

$42.2M — $29.4M — $26.0M — $16.2M

N=1,015 celebrities
(based on 203 entertainment attorneys)

N=1,015 celebrities
(based on 203 entertainment attorneys)

Like other wealthy sub-segments we have studied, men are better represented than women. Roughly three-quarters of our celebrity sample was male, which is consistent with other high-net-worth populations such as business owners and private jet owners (Exhibit 1.4). One difference for celebrities, however, is wealth by gender. It's clear than some professions are more lucrative than others, but our research shows that financial success within a given field (hedge fund managers, for example) is fairly consistent across genders.

In the case of celebrity wealth, men have higher net worths with average assets of US$39 million and median assets of US$26 million compared to an average net worth of US$30 million and median net worth of US$21 million for women (Exhibit 1.5), perhaps an indication that the gender inequities that plague other industries are an issue in the entertainment field as well.

EXHIBIT 1.4: *Gender*

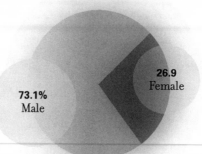

26.9
Female

73.1%
Male

N=1,015 celebrities
(based on 203 entertainment attorneys)

EXHIBIT 1.5: *Wealth by Gender*

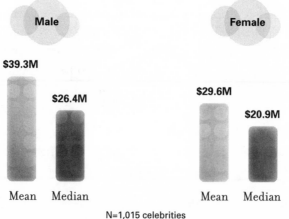

Male

Female

$39.3M

$26.4M

$29.6M

$20.9M

Mean   Median   Mean   Median

N=1,015 celebrities
(based on 203 entertainment attorneys)

Another major difference for celebrities, as compared to the larger affluent population, is their ability to amass meaningful assets at a much younger age than is typically possible in other professions. About half of the celebrities studied were below the age of 40, which means they have longer to live and work and may find that their lifestyle, financial, and professional priorities shift over time (Exhibit 1.6).

EXHIBIT 1.6: *Age*

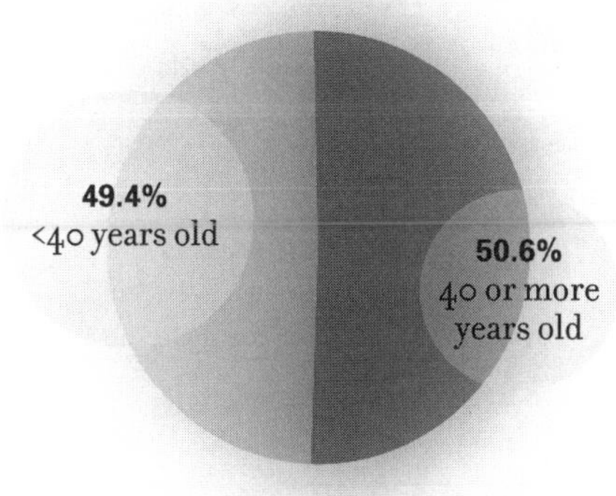

49.4%
<40 years old

50.6%
40 or more
years old

N=1,015 celebrities
(based on 203 entertainment attorneys)

Interestingly, the difference in overall level of wealth was less pronounced when viewed by age. Younger celebrities have an average net worth of US$34 million and median net worth of US$23 million, while older celebrities had an average net worth of US$39 million and median assets of US$27 million (Exhibit 1.7).

EXHIBIT 1.7: *Wealth by Age*

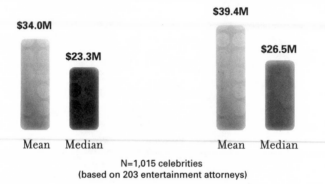

< 40 years old   40 or more years old

$34.0M $23.3M $39.4M $26.5M

Mean   Median   Mean   Median

N=1,015 celebrities
(based on 203 entertainment attorneys)

PERSPECTIVES ON THE BUSINESS

Entertainment is a notoriously fickle business; what's hot one day can be considered passé just days later. And fans can be a source of both elation and misery. Entertainers have multiple audiences to consider and must clear numerous business hurdles before their "product" is available to the general public. For almost all, or 95 percent, of status-oriented celebrities the stress associated with a constant spotlight and need for reputation management is significant. Slightly fewer craft-oriented celebrities, about 78 percent, have a similar perspective (Exhibit 1.8).

EXHIBIT 1.8: *A Very Stressful Business*

94.3%

77.8%

88.9%

Status-
oriented

Craft-
oriented

Weighted
Average

N=1,015 celebrities
(based on 203 entertainment attorneys)

Every move a celebrity makes can be monitored and, frequently, the decisions they make are second-guessed — an environment that can feel unfriendly and uncertain. For some celebrities, particularly those focused on status, a fear of failure is overwhelming. This is a concern for about three-quarters of status-oriented celebs, compared to just 36 percent of their craft-oriented peers (Exhibit 1.9). The higher concern among status-oriented professionals is logical given how dependent their success is on the perceptions of others.

EXHIBIT 1.9: *Intense Fear of Failing*

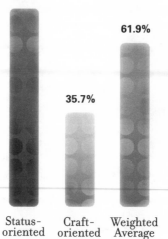

N=1,015 celebrities
(based on 203 entertainment attorneys)

Few celebrities, in total just 36 percent, pay significant attention to the business side of their careers, preferring instead to turn all those responsibilities over to managers, agents, publicists, financial advisors, and the like (Exhibit 1.10). However, roughly twice as many status-oriented celebs were involved in the business aspects of their career when compared to their craft-oriented counterparts.

EXHIBIT 1.10: *Focused on the Business Side of Their Career*

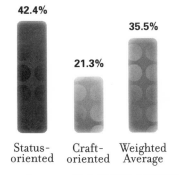

42.4%

35.5%

21.3%

Status-oriented   Craft-oriented   Weighted Average

N=1,015 celebrities
(based on 203 entertainment attorneys)

Despite a seeming lack of interest in business matters, the number of celebrities that think of themselves as a business entity is fairly sizeable at 60 percent (Exhibit 1.11). The link between the professional and the fiscal results is acknowledged – especially by status-oriented celebs – but limited interest in the business side of things means very few are actively managing and advancing the connection in any proactive way.

EXHIBIT 1.11: *See Themselves as a Business*

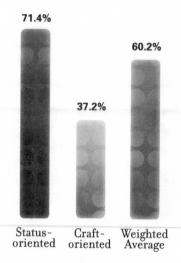

71.4%

60.2%

37.2%

Status-   Craft-   Weighted
oriented   oriented   Average

N=1,015 celebrities
(based on 203 entertainment attorneys)

The right attitude can make a big difference in most situations — and getting rich is no different. Celebrities that perceived themselves as a business were wealthier than those professionals that did not share that perspective (Exhibit 1.12).

EXHIBIT 1.12: *Wealth by Business Perception*

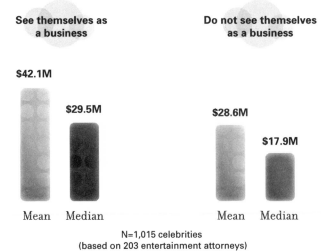

N=1,015 celebrities
(based on 203 entertainment attorneys)

Overall, about half of the celebrities studied acknowledge the uncertainty of an entertainment career. More than three-quarters of craft-oriented professionals recognize that their careers could be short-lived, a figure that's not surprising given their more intense focus and dedication to a single, specialized area (Exhibit 1.13). Just 36 percent of status-oriented professionals believe this to be the case, which may indicate a willingness to branch into other activities that can extend a career.

EXHIBIT 1.13: *Understand Their Careers Might Have a Limited Lifespan*

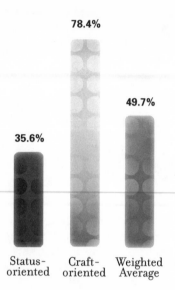

78.4%

49.7%

35.6%

Status-
oriented

Craft-
oriented

Weighted
Average

N=1,015 celebrities
(based on 203 entertainment attorneys)

IMPLICATIONS FOR CELEBRITIES AND THEIR ADVISORS

The psychographic segments we've discussed — status-oriented versus craft-oriented — are guidelines to understanding a complex and intricate type of professional. Some celebrities may strongly identify with the descriptions, while others may recognize some qualities in themselves or none at all. At a minimum, they are a point of reference that can help clarify the motivations and priorities of an entertainment professional, along with the opportunities and limitations that can accompany specific mindsets. For both celebrities and their advisors, the knowledge of these segments can be useful when navigating significant business, financial, and lifestyle decisions.

BOTH SIDES

of Fame

AT A GLANCE

Fame has advantages and drawbacks, and how celebrities perceived the benefits and detriments was a function of their orientation to the industry.

Status-oriented celebs view recognition from fans, the media, and peers as one of the greatest advantages of their celebrity status.

They also saw more value in the rewards of celebrity – such as preferential access, treatment, and financial opportunities – and the ability to influence youngsters, political agendas, and charitable causes.

The top three benefits for craft-oriented professionals were the freedom to do what they love, the recognition of their talent, and the independence enabled by fame and success.

On the downside, the loss of privacy and career influence, psychological disorders, and security concerns were the most negative aspects of fame for status-oriented celebs.

They are also concerned about the impact their fame had on lifestyle expectations and expenditures, the unity of their family, and their own sense of normalcy.

Craft-oriented professionals were less concerned across the board, but also believed that fame could lead to unpleasant results with personal security and mental stability.

It's commonly said that there are two sides to every story and celebrities clearly see both the positive and negative aspects of their fame and wealth. In this chapter, we'll take a closer look at the advantages — the many things that can make being a talented and recognized professional an enjoyable and rewarding experience — as well as the disadvantages — those aspects that can have a negative and pervasive impact on a celebrity's life, relationships, and career.

THE UPSIDE OF FAME

Most people would agree that being a celebrity has its perks, and when asked about the advantages of their careers, most wealthy celebrities can point to a few things they appreciate. However, as with wealth, a celeb's career orientation had a big influence on how certain benefits were perceived and valued.

INCENTIVES

We've all read the stories about the swag available to celebrities that attend film festivals and promotional events – the chance to pick up the latest styles of sunglasses, jeans, pocketbooks, and cell phones, among other things, in the privacy of a hotel suite or a VIP-only room. In recent years, the gift baskets at awards ceremonies were so extreme that the IRS threatened to include a tax declaration along with the certificates for week-long stays at destination resorts, jewelry, and the like. But free stuff isn't the only incentive that accompanies fame, or the only reward that celebrities value.

In every case, status-oriented celebrities were more likely – sometimes two to three times more likely – to recognize and appreciate the incentives of their fame than craft-oriented celebrities were (Exhibit 2.1). The benefits they felt were most advantageous were access to new and potentially lucrative financial opportunities, the ability to live a life of luxury, and VIP access to powerful people and desirable places. The benefit that revealed the greatest difference in thinking between the status-oriented and the craft-oriented individuals was receiving preferential treatment by law enforcement and the judicial system, which was a worthwhile bonus of fame for more than three times as many status-oriented celebs.

EXHIBIT 2.1: *The Incentives of Fame*

BENEFIT	STATUS-ORIENTED	CRAFT-ORIENTED	WEIGHTED AVERAGE
Additional financial opportunities	80.2%	43.8%	68.3%
A luxurious lifestyle	76.4%	27.6%	60.4%
Are showered with perks	49.3%	20.4%	39.8%
Preferential access to people and places	70.4%	35.4%	58.9%
The best health care available	49.6%	25.2%	41.6%
Preferential treatment by the police and the courts	61.4%	18.3%	47.3%

N = 1,015 celebrities (based on 203 entertainment attorneys)

ATTENTION

Given the international obsession with fame, one of the major byproducts of celebrity is being in the spotlight. While a lack of privacy may bother some people (see below), nearly all celebrities – regardless of their career orientation – felt that recognition of their talent was the best aspect of being famous (Exhibit 2.2). The attention from adoring fans was a big plus – a way to stay in the public eye and make more money – for a similarly high number, 95 percent, of status-oriented professionals, while just 35 percent of craft-oriented celebs felt this way.

EXHIBIT 2.2: *The Attention From Fame*

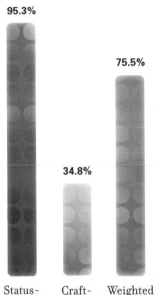

Recognition of their talent

99.3% 98.8% 99.1%

Status- Craft- Weighted
oriented oriented Average

Adoring fans

95.3%

75.5%

34.8%

Status- Craft- Weighted
oriented oriented Average

PERSONAL FULFILLMENT

Celebrities or otherwise, most people aspire to personal fulfillment and satisfaction. However, given the highly-individualized nature of these goals, the degree to which something contributes to satisfaction will vary from person to person. And the same is true of celebrities, with craft-oriented celebs prizing different things than their status-oriented peers. Almost all, 99 percent, of those more focused on their craft cherished the ability to do what they love and 90 percent took pleasure in the independence their fame imparted compared to only three-quarters of status-oriented celebs (Exhibit 2.3). Conversely, the ability to have control over their lives was important to twice as many status-oriented individuals when compared to craft-oriented celebrities, and just 36 percent of all celebrities felt strongly about using their fame to help family and friends.

EXHIBIT 2.3: *Fulfilling Aspects of Fame*

BENEFIT	STATUS-ORIENTED	CRAFT-ORIENTED	WEIGHTED AVERAGE
Independence	77.1%	89.5%	81.2%
Able to do what the love doing	75.2%	98.5%	82.9%
Have considerable control over their lives	60.3%	30.0%	50.3%
Able to help family and friends	32.6%	44.1%	36.4%

N = 1,015 celebrities (based on 203 entertainment attorneys)

INFLUENCE

Many celebrities take their role in the spotlight seriously and want to use their notoriety to make a difference. Some choose to support specific agendas – medical, political, religious, for example – by raising awareness or funding certain initiatives. Others realize that some fans, especially children and teenagers, view them as role models and want to emulate their behavior. As with rewards, status-oriented celebs felt the opportunities that accompany their fame to influence society were bigger advantages than did craft-oriented celebrities (Exhibit 2.4). The ability to act as a role model was perceived as a benefit by 91 percent of celebrities focused on the status of their careers, and 79 percent valued the opportunity to create a professional legacy, either through their body of work, a private foundation, or another philanthropic endeavor. Using celebrity to have a positive impact on a charity was gratifying for 69 percent of status-oriented individuals; these types of activities can provide the additional benefits of certain tax advantages for contributions, a halo effect for high-profile volunteers and donors, and added media attention for worthwhile causes. Lastly, almost half of the status-oriented group felt the chance to influence politics was a positive benefit of fame.

The responses tied to the craft-oriented segment revealed a far different mindset. Slightly less than two-thirds found the opportunity to leave a professional legacy a plus, and 57 percent liked the ability to have a positive impact on charitable causes. Just 39 percent of this group saw themselves as role models for the population at large and even fewer, 19 percent, viewed the chance to exert political influence as a bonus. These results further emphasize the single-minded priorities of craft-oriented professionals and their limited interest in the ancillary aspects of celebrity.

EXHIBIT 2.4: *Using Fame as an Influencer*

BENEFIT	STATUS-ORIENTED	CRAFT-ORIENTED	WEIGHTED AVERAGE
Can act as a role model for others	91.1%	39.3%	74.1%
Can influence politics	46.8%	19.2%	37.7%
Make a major difference by supporting charities	68.8%	56.5%	64.7%
Create a professional legacy	78.7%	60.7%	72.8%

N = 1,015 celebrities (based on 203 entertainment attorneys)

THE DOWNSIDE OF FAME

The Greek folk hero, Aesop, best known for his moral fables wrote, "Every truth has two sides," and that is surely the case with fame. In addition to the many perks we discussed previously, there is a downside as well, and most celebrities were very aware of the aspects they like least about their lives in the spotlight.

BEING A TARGET

Despite the importance of adoring fans and receiving high recognition for their talents, the lack of privacy and anonymity that accompanies a successful career in entertainment is an issue for many celebrities; it is a concern for more than half of craft-oriented celebrities and almost three-quarters of status-oriented celebrities (Exhibit 2.5). Far fewer felt their public persona meant they would be taken advantage of by the professionals that advise them on the many facets of their careers; just 17 percent of craft-oriented celebs and 31 percent of status-oriented celebs.

EXHIBIT 2.5: *Targeted by Fame*

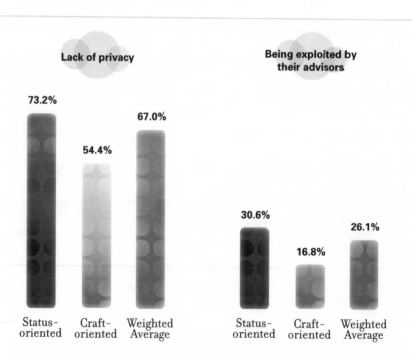

Lack of privacy

73.2% — Status-oriented
54.4% — Craft-oriented
67.0% — Weighted Average

Being exploited by their advisors

30.6% — Status-oriented
16.8% — Craft-oriented
26.1% — Weighted Average

N=1,015 celebrities
(based on 203 entertainment attorneys)

THE PSYCHOLOGICAL IMPACT

The negative impact that fame can have on one's mindset and mental health can be significant, although in most cases, status-oriented celebs were more likely to feel the burden than their craft-oriented peers – not surprisingly given the pressure they place on themselves to maintain a specific image. For roughly three-quarters of status-oriented celebs, fame led to an unrealistic sense of entitlement – perhaps a side effect of being catered to by employees, fans, and the media – and either anxiety, depression or both (Exhibit 2.6). For just over than half, it led to some form of substance abuse and the urge to self-medicate with pharmaceutical or street drugs, which can be related to the aforementioned anxiety and depression and compounded by the increased exposure and access a celebrity often has to recreational substances. Eating disorders were another negative side effect of being a celebrity for a smaller number, 35 percent.

Far fewer craft-oriented professionals identified with any of these aspects, with one exception – anxiety and depression. Almost 80 percent of these celebs saw it as the worst psychological aspect of fame.

EXHIBIT 2.6: *Psychological Impact of Fame*

ISSUE	STATUS-ORIENTED	CRAFT-ORIENTED	WEIGHTED AVERAGE
An unrealistic sense of entitlement	75.8%	12.9%	55.2%
Drug and alcohol abuse	56.3%	14.4%	42.6%
Eating disorders	34.8%	11.7%	27.2%
Anxiety/depression	74.2%	78.3%	65.7%
Self-medicating	57.3%	21.9%	49.7%
N = 1,015 celebrities (based on 203 entertainment attorneys)			

FAMILY MATTERS

To some degree, people that exist in the limelight expect their lives to be under constant scrutiny, but often that scrutiny and pressure is unfairly extended to others in their inner circle, particularly family and friends who may or may not be in the business. Again, status-oriented celebs felt a stronger impact, with about 60 percent concerned about divorce and raising their children in an environment with skewed values (Exhibit 2.7). About half the number of craft-oriented professionals felt the same way, demonstrating recognition that their careers could have a detrimental effect on their families, but to a much lesser degree than their status-conscious counterparts.

EXHIBIT 2.7: *Fame's Impact on Family*

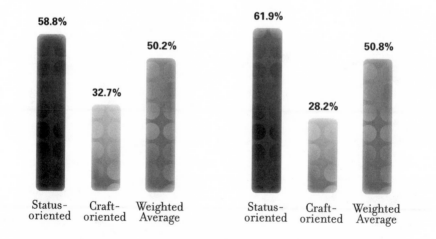

Their children growing up without meaningful values

58.8%
32.7%
50.2%

Status-oriented   Craft-oriented   Weighted Average

Divorce

61.9%
28.2%
50.8%

Status-oriented   Craft-oriented   Weighted Average

N=1,015 celebrities
(based on 203 entertainment attorneys)

LIFESTYLE MAINTENANCE

It stands to reason that status-oriented celebrities will want, and even feel obligated, to live lavishly. It's a benchmark for success, expected by their peers, and support network, and helps garner the attention of fans and the media – all important components of establishing stature in an unpredictable industry. Nearly 70 percent recognized the considerable cost of their current lifestyles and 60 percent felt the pressure to maintain a rapidly escalating lifestyle (Exhibit 2.8). Again, just a fraction of the number of craft-oriented celebrities felt the same way. Lifestyle costs and lifestyle expansion were meaningful issues for just 26 percent and 21 percent, respectively; these numbers underscore the fact that craft-oriented professionals are less concerned with the conventional trappings of fame.

EXHIBIT 2.8: *Lifestyle Concerns*

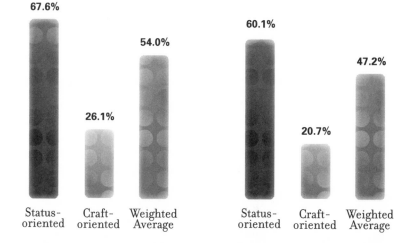

Paying for their current lifestyle

67.6% Status-oriented
26.1% Craft-oriented
54.0% Weighted Average

Maintaining an expanding lifestyle

60.1% Status-oriented
20.7% Craft-oriented
47.2% Weighted Average

N=1,015 celebrities
(based on 203 entertainment attorneys)

ANOTHER REASON TO WORRY — NO CAREER CONTROL

A number of other issues regularly surface in our discussions with wealthy celebrities that we chose to probe further in our study. The first is a sense that they do not have sufficient involvement in the overall direction of their career. It often seems that celebrities are surrounded by more people than high-ranking politicians or CEOs of powerful corporations — and these people insert themselves into everything from the most menial task (ordering coffee) to an issue of vital importance (contract negotiations). This means that someone in the cadre of professionals that advise them, such as publicists, stylists, nutritionists, trainers, agents, or members of their entourage, will have a say as they hone their expertise, make creative choices, and attempt to advance their careers. Lack of career influence and control was an issue for roughly three-quarters of status-oriented celebs and 62 percent of craft-oriented individuals (Exhibit 2.9).

EXHIBIT 2.9: *Feel They Do Not Have "Real" Control Over Their Careers*

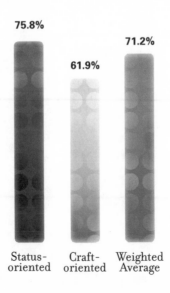

75.8%		71.2%
	61.9%	
Status-oriented	Craft-oriented	Weighted Average

N=1,015 celebrities
(based on 203 entertainment attorneys)

PERSONAL SECURITY

Through our ongoing work with wealthy individuals and families, we know that personal security has emerged as the number one concern and, not surprisingly, the larger the fortune, the greater the apprehension. Add a high-profile job to the mix and crimes such as kidnapping, stalking, random or planned attacks, identity theft, and robbery become a very real possibility. Slightly less than half of both segments felt that their personal wealth could attract some undesirable elements (Exhibit 2.10). Understandably, more than 80 percent of status-oriented celebs were concerned that their fame made them a target (versus just 29 percent of craft-oriented celebs), as they probably spend proportionately more time in the public eye than their fellow entertainers.

EXHIBIT 2.10: *The Personal Security Impact of Fame & Fortune*

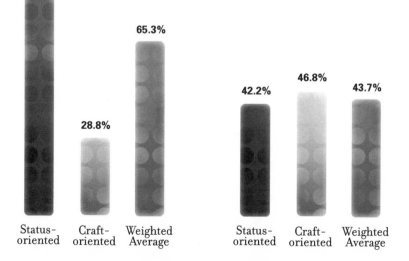

Their fame makes them a target

83.1% — Status-oriented
28.8% — Craft-oriented
65.3% — Weighted Average

Their wealth makes them a target

42.2% — Status-oriented
46.8% — Craft-oriented
43.7% — Weighted Average

N=1,015 celebrities
(based on 203 entertainment attorneys)

The majority of celebrities felt the situation had gotten worse over the past year and would continue to escalate – but status-conscious celebs were far more attuned to the security risks of their fame than craft-oriented celebrities (Exhibit 2.11).

EXHIBIT 2.11: *The Personal Security Impact of Fame & Fortune*

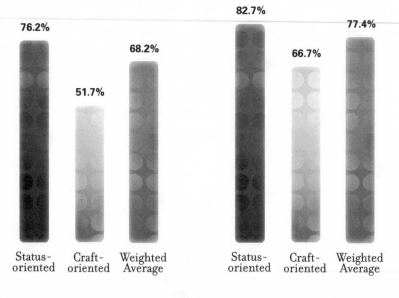

More concerned than last year

76.2% — Status-oriented
51.7% — Craft-oriented
68.2% — Weighted Average

The situation will only worsen

82.7% — Status-oriented
66.7% — Craft-oriented
77.4% — Weighted Average

N=1,015 celebrities
(based on 203 entertainment attorneys)

Although security concerns were high among most celebrities, very few had hired a security consultant in the previous two years. Just 44 percent of status-oriented professionals and 30 percent of craft-oriented professionals had done so (Exhibit 2.12).

EXHIBIT 2.12: *Hired a Security Consultant in the Last 2 Years*

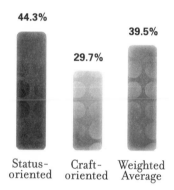

44.3%

39.5%

29.7%

Status-
oriented

Craft-
oriented

Weighted
Average

N=1,015 celebrities
(based on 203 entertainment attorneys)

IMPLICATIONS FOR CELEBRITIES AND THEIR ADVISORS

High profile individuals must be aware of the constant struggle required to maintain a life and career in the spotlight, and they have to be prepared to work hard to find the necessary balance to make fame work. This may depend on great personal discipline as well as the assistance of friends, colleagues, and advisors. The professionals that provide support and guidance to celebrities must be attuned to the polarity of their clients' lives and continually modify their services and interactions in ways that best meet the current situation.

3

BETWEEN
the Sheets

**AT A
GLANCE**

When it comes to sexual activity, most celebrities believe that their wealth and social status have had a positive impact.

Overall, the status-oriented professionals were more likely to have capitalized on their celebrity to enrich their sexual lives in a variety of ways.

Status-oriented professionals were more likely to value sex as part of their lifestyle, and to credit their fame and fortune for affording them a better sex life.

They also had more affairs, slept with more people and hired more sex professionals than their peers.

Craft-oriented celebs value high-quality sexual interactions over sheer quantity, a perspective that also extends to their professional choices.

We already know

that money can buy access to the things that engender excitement and satisfaction, however that may be defined and interpreted. And in a recent survey of multimillionaires, we learned that ultra-wealthy people believe their wealth has had a positive impact on their sex lives, enabling them to have better partners, higher-quality interactions, and more adventurous and exotic sex. Our goal with this survey was to determine whether the element of fame has a similar impact on sex for celebrities, and so we included a series of questions about sexual attitudes and behavior.

Nearly all the survey respondents were in a committed relationship whether with a spouse or a significant other. Slightly more men than women, 97 to 91 percent, had a life partner (Exhibits 3.1 and 3.2).

EXHIBIT 3.1: *Have a Life Partner by Orientation*

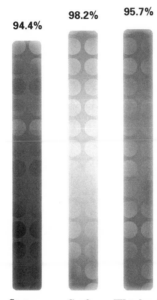

94.4%   98.2%   95.7%

Status-   Craft-   Weighted
oriented   oriented   Average

N=1,015 celebrities
(based on 203 entertainment attorneys)

EXHIBIT 3.2: *Have a Life Partner by Gender*

97.3%   91.2%   95.7%

Male   Female   Weighted
Average

N=1,015 celebrities
(based on 203 entertainment attorneys)

PHILANDERING

Of the celebrities with a life partner, a number have had affairs outside the relationship and status-oriented celebrities were twice as likely to have engaged in an affair than craft-oriented celebrities (Exhibit 3.3).

EXHIBIT 3.3: *Have Had an Affair by Orientation*

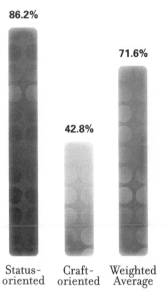

N=971 celebrities
(based on 203 entertainment attorneys)

When viewed by gender, female celebs were more likely to have had an affair than male celebs (Exhibit 3.4). This is consistent with other wealthy populations, which may indicate that fame enhances the liberating and empowering effects that money has on women.

EXHIBIT 3.4: *Have Had an Affair by Gender*

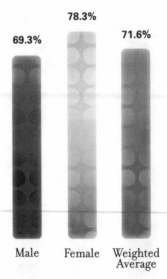

Male Female Weighted Average

N=971 celebrities
(based on 203 entertainment attorneys)

A TOP PRIORITY

Sex is important for the majority of celebrities, but to a much greater degree among status-oriented celebs than their craft-oriented counterparts (Exhibit 3.5). This is further evidence that craft-oriented professionals are less enticed by the perks of fame and activities that fall squarely outside the scope of their chosen trade.

EXHIBIT 3.5: *Sex is Very or Extremely Important by Orientation*

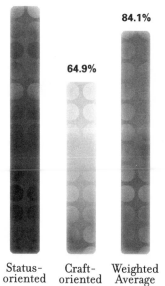

93.5%

84.1%

64.9%

Status-oriented   Craft-oriented   Weighted Average

N=1,015 celebrities
(based on 203 entertainment attorneys)

Given the statistics on affairs, it's not surprising that more high-profile women felt sex was an important part of their life and lifestyle than men did (Exhibit 3.6).

EXHIBIT 3.6: *Sex is Very or Extremely Important by Gender*

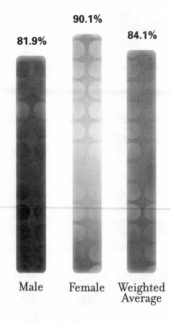

90.1%

81.9%

84.1%

Male   Female   Weighted Average

N=1,015 celebrities
(based on 203 entertainment attorneys)

Of the celebrities that thought sex was important, most felt that their money and recognition had helped them to lead a better sex life than they would have had otherwise. The breakdown by segment is consistent, with 93 percent of status-oriented celebs and 61 percent of craft-oriented in accord (Exhibit 3.7).

EXHIBIT 3.7:  *Better Sex by Orientation*

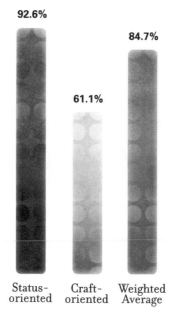

92.6%

84.7%

61.1%

Status-oriented   Craft-oriented   Weighted Average

N=854 celebrities
(based on 203 entertainment attorneys)

Again, more women than men felt the advantages of fame and fortune extended to the bedroom; this is the case for nearly all female celebrities compared to 80 percent of male celebs (Exhibit 3.8).

EXHIBIT 3.8: *Better Sex by Gender*

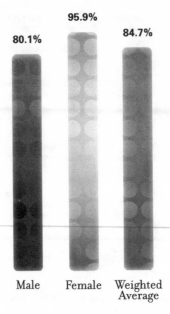

95.9%

80.1%

84.7%

Male Female Weighted
Average

N=854 celebrities
(based on 203 entertainment attorneys)

Better, of course, is a subjective and highly variable term, so we delved deeper to uncover the reasons behind the perceived improvement. Higher-quality sex was far and away the number one driver behind a better sex life for craft-oriented individuals — not a stretch given their focus on the quality of their professional performances (Exhibit 3.9). The adventurous and exotic nature of their sexual activities was a contributor to better sex for less than half that number.

The status-conscious celebs were also appreciative of the higher-quality sex, but to a lesser degree than their craft-oriented peers. But for a large group, 79 percent, the ability to be more daring and experimental was a factor in attaining a better sex life, as was the variety of sexual partners for 63 percent. On a relative basis, fewer celebs overall felt the frequency of sex was a component of a better sex life as access to willing participants was presumably not a problem.

EXHIBIT 3.9: *Reasons for Better Sex by Orientation*

REASONS FOR BETTER SEX	STATUS-ORIENTED	CRAFT-ORIENTED	WEIGHTED AVERAGE
Higher quality	90.2%	79.9%	81.7%
More frequent	22.0%	36.9%	34.2%
More partners	18.2%	62.8%	54.6%
More adventurous and/or exotic	42.4%	79.4%	72.6%

N = 723 celebrities (based on 203 entertainment attorneys)

The elements of better sex varied when segmented by gender. For a large majority of both men and women, the focus is on high-quality sexual interactions, but general agreement ended there. Almost all female celebrities, 95 percent, felt more adventurous and exotic sex was the greatest driver behind their superior sex lives, while just 62 percent of males felt similarly (Exhibit 3.10). By contrast, male celebs were far more likely than women to identify the number of partners and the frequency of sexual activity as factors.

It's also worth noting that there are some consistencies between celebrities and the rest of the affluent universe when it comes to the definition of better sex – the same things that were important to the female celebrities in our study were rated similarly by other wealthy females we have surveyed, and the same was true when it came to the male perspective. The major difference is the degree to which men value the number of sexual partners and interactions they have. About three-quarters of wealthy males in a previous study said frequency and variety were benefits of wealth and significant contributors to their definition of better sex, while the number of occurrences was relevant for just 42 percent of male celebs.

EXHIBIT 3.10: *Reasons for Better Sex by Gender*

REASONS FOR BETTER SEX	MALE	FEMALE	WEIGHTED AVERAGE
Higher quality	79.5%	86.4%	81.7%
More frequent	42.3%	17.4%	34.2%
More partners	67.4%	28.4%	54.6%
More adventurous and/or exotic	61.8%	94.9%	72.6%

N = 723 celebrities (based on 203 entertainment attorneys)

SEX IN THE AIR

Just half of the celebrities in our survey sample were members of the well known, and somewhat notorious, mile-high club (Exhibit 3.11). More than four times as many status-oriented celebrities than their craft-oriented colleagues had engaged in sexual activity in a plane (Exhibit 3.12). The gender differences remained pronounced as well, with almost 70 percent of female celebrities and just 44 percent of male celebrities following suit (Exhibit 3.13).

EXHIBIT 3.11: *Members of the Mile High Club*

50.4%
Members of
Mile High Club

N=1,006 celebrities
(based on 203 entertainment attorneys)

EXHIBIT 3.12: *Members of the Mile High Club by Orientation*

67.2%

15.1%

Craft-
oriented

Status-
oriented

N=1,006 celebrities
(based on 203 entertainment attorneys)

EXHIBIT 3.13: *Members of the Mile High Club by Gender*

68.9%

43.5%

Male

Female

N=1,006 celebrities
(based on 203 entertainment attorneys)

ECONOMIES OF SCALE

Musicians reveled in the groupie culture long before the advent of rock 'n roll, and now other types of celebrities and entertainers are using their notoriety to enhance their sex lives. Status-oriented celebrities had slept with significantly more people than their craft-oriented peers — almost seven times more on an average basis and more than three times the median number (Exhibit 3.14). Again, this was not surprising given the status-oriented celebs strong interest in the profile and perks associated with an entertainment career and the craft-oriented celebs' strong passion for the profession. When segmented by gender, male and female celebs had a similar numbers of sexual partners (Exhibit 3.15).

EXHIBIT 3.14: *Number of Sex Partners by Orientation*

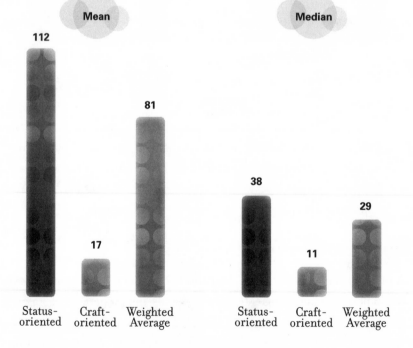

Mean

112

81

17

Status-oriented   Craft-oriented   Weighted Average

Median

38

11

29

Status-oriented   Craft-oriented   Weighted Average

N=1,006 celebrities
(based on 203 entertainment attorneys)

EXHIBIT 3.15: *Number of Sex Partners by Gender*

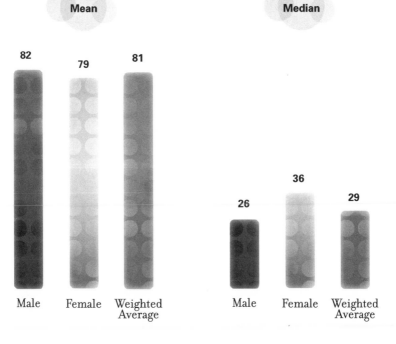

Mean

Median

82 79 81

36 29
26

Male Female Weighted Average   Male Female Weighted Average

N=1,006 celebrities
(based on 203 entertainment attorneys)

Another interesting finding is that less than 1 percent of our survey sample had never had sex — just nine of the 1,015 individuals in our study were virgins. Perhaps most telling is that they were all male and all craft-oriented in nature, ranging in age from 28 to 46 years old.

TURNING TO PROFESSIONALS

A relatively small portion of celebrities had paid a professional for sex; just 3 percent of craft-oriented professionals and 20 percent of status-oriented professionals (Exhibit 3.16). For some of the celebrities that did, the appeal was having a "no strings attached" experience. Notwithstanding the importance of sex and the incidence of affairs among women, they were less likely than men to have hired a professional (Exhibit 3.17).

EXHIBIT 3.16: *Paid for Sex by Orientation*

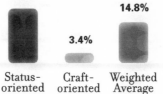

20.2%

14.8%

3.4%

Status-oriented Craft-oriented Weighted Average

N=1,015 celebrities
(based on 203 entertainment attorneys)

EXHIBIT 3.17: *Paid for Sex by Gender*

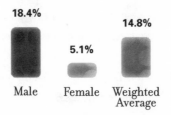

18.4%

14.8%

5.1%

Male Female Weighted Average

N=1,015 celebrities
(based on 203 entertainment attorneys)

ONE MORE CONCERN

There's no question that a bounty of sex can be enjoyable, but there can be unpleasant drawbacks too. Exposure to sexually transmitted diseases was an issue for one-quarter of status-oriented individuals and 9 percent of craft-oriented celebs (Exhibit 3.18).

EXHIBITS 3.18: *Sexually Transmitted Diseases*

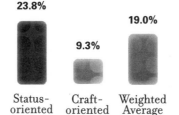

23.8%

19.0%

9.3%

Status-
oriented

Craft-
oriented

Weighted
Average

N=1,015 celebrities
(based on 203 entertainment attorneys)

IMPLICATIONS FOR CELEBRITIES AND THEIR ADVISORS

For most people, sex is a highly personal, and usually private, activity. For others, it is one facet of their public persona and an interesting byproduct of a high profile career. Celebrities, if inclined, can leverage their fame and stature into a more satisfying sex life. Females, in particular, seem more empowered by their fame and wealth than men when it comes to sexual freedom. But taking these results at face value overlooks a bigger implication, and that is that the sexual behavior of celebrities and their perspectives of how fame and fortune have impacted their sex lives can be taken as a proxy for the other activities that can be used by high profile individuals to enhance their lifestyles and their careers. Celebrities should be attuned to the empowering nature of their fame and wealth, and advisors should keep an eye out for unique opportunities that can help their clients find even greater success and fulfillment.

CENTERED FOR *Success*

Based on our experience with the wealthy, it's very easy for successful, affluent individuals to succumb to the pressure and demands around them. This is especially so for individuals in high-stress roles such as hedge fund managers, when a single decision can impact hundreds of other affluent individuals and a single trade can result in a gain or loss of many millions of dollars. This is also the case with celebrities, individuals who are at the center of an inordinate amount of attention and activity that can be distracting and overwhelming, and whose audiences and employers are vocal, opinionated and, often, unforgiving.

Derailing — or losing that essential focus — can have a negative impact that reverberates widely. It can cause self-esteem and motivation to suffer. It can further complicate personal and professional relationships. It can hamper progress and effectiveness, smother proficiency, and even color a person's ability to grasp and analyze information. This, in turn, can have a material and detrimental effect on that individual's success — the success derived from the fulfillment, stature, and advancement of his or her career, as well as financial success.

It's easy to grasp the link between derailing and the strain and anxiety that accompany a high-stress, high-profile vocation. But it's important to recognize that derailing can occur at any time and, increasingly, we are seeing it occur when professionals are at the pinnacle of their careers.

A VERY STRESSFUL BUSINESS

We've already established that being a celebrity can be stressful and that celebrityhood, for all of its perks, also carries its share of hassles and shortcoming. This situation can be further exacerbated by the growing feeling among celebrities that they have no control over their careers. For many, this leads to a search for ways to minimize the effects of stress, often through activities as varied as exercise, meditation, family-time, therapy, medication or drugs, hobbies, life-coaches, alcohol, religion, serial dating or, simply more work. For some, this feeling of being out of control leads to a cycle of negative behavior that is difficult to break.

The individuals that fare best in these environments are those that are able to stay centered. By centered we mean that they are:

| In touch with themselves and their responsibilities;

| Clear about their unique skills and talents and how to best leverage them toward a specific set of goals;

| Able to focus on the key challenges and obligations in front of them; and

| Armed with the resolve, confidence and determination to do so.

In essence, centered people find the focus – as needed – to keep their lives and careers on track.

Unfortunately, very few celebrities can be described as centered, and this has a direct correlation to their emotional satisfaction and career success. Just 22 percent of the celebrities in our study were highly centered, with the other 78 percent much less so (Exhibit 4.1).

EXHIBIT 4.1: *Degree of Centeredness*

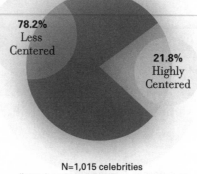

78.2%
Less
Centered

21.8%
Highly
Centered

N=1,015 celebrities
(based on 203 entertainment attorneys)

As discussed in *Chapter 2: Both Sides of Fame,* 71 percent of all celebrities feel they have no real control over their careers. Understandably, those celebrities that are highly centered are more likely to feel they have a say in how their career evolves. Three-quarters of highly centered celebs believe they are in control – a significant improvement over (and a direct contrast to) the sentiments of the larger group (Exhibit 4.2). Unfortunately, celebrities with a less centered approach were the most discouraged – just 6 percent of them felt they had any control over their careers – an emotional state that can snowball and make it even harder to find grounding and focus.

EXHIBIT 4.2: *Feel They Do Not Have "Real" Control Over Their Careers by Centeredness*

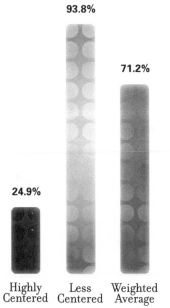

93.8%

71.2%

24.9%

| Highly | Less | Weighted |
| Centered | Centered | Average |

N=1,015 celebrities
(based on 203 entertainment attorneys)

HIGHLY CENTERED CELEBRITIES ARE WEALTHIER

For celebrities, being centered has many advantages that can increase the overall quality of their life. One of those advantages is greater wealth; celebs that were highly centered had significantly greater net worth of those that were less centered (Exhibit 4.3). Without question, a larger bank account can be a nice byproduct of a centered approach.

EXHIBIT 4.3: *Wealth by Centeredness*

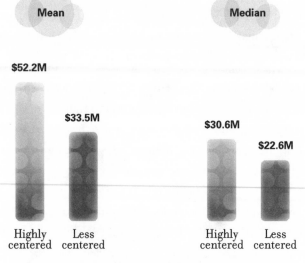

N=1,015 celebrities
(based on 203 entertainment attorneys)

BECOMING AND STAYING CENTERED

A large part of our practices has become one-on-one work with wealthy and established clients to help them adopt the right mindset and proficiencies – and achieve a more centered approach – in pursuit of even greater professional and financial success.

Through an empirical process, we have identified that highly successful people in all fields draw upon some combination of three primary elements to reach their objectives:

| Special skills and talents.

| A great deal of persistence and hard work.

| A little bit of luck.

As noted above, an important part of a centered approach is recognizing what your unique skills and talents are and how to best use them, acknowledging the commitment and effort that you give to your career, and understanding that things like timing and destiny can often play an important role in the way that events unfold. A heightened awareness of these things makes it easier to leverage your abilities and act on opportunities when they present themselves.

Many celebrities allow themselves to become weighed down by the stresses of the business, succumbing to the industry clichés of drink, drugs and divorce. Others employ more productive approaches to handling the stress, like surrounding themselves with people who understand what they are confronting and can provide the appropriate degree and type of support. We refer to this role as an "angst buffer," and it is usually filled by life partners, friends, family members, spiritualists, and therapists. At other times, business coaches can provide solutions to productively mitigate stress, but they must specialize in the issues unique to the entertainment world to be truly effective.

Coaching is a complex discipline as it draws on time-tested principles and incorporates many systematic processes, but must be fully customized around the affluent individual in order to achieve specific results. We believe that coaching celebrities should result in them staying centered and capitalizing on their unique talents and abilities *no matter what is happening around them.*

Part of the process, when working with successful celebrities, is to identify and explore a range of cognitive and physical techniques that can yield the focus and execution needed to excel and, ultimately, deliver career satisfaction and fulfillment. One example is the use of the ancient Hindu and Buddhist practices of Tantra. Through the coaching process it is often possible to build on your unique talents and abilities and develop new skills that can make you even more successful.

By staying centered, it is possible to withstand the many difficulties and distractions that accompany a career in entertainment and eventually achieve a higher level of success. Moreover, research shows that celebrities who build careers around their distinct abilities and talents, and remain focused on their personal and professional goals and responsibilities have total net worths among the industry's top 10 percent.

THE RIPPLE EFFECT

There's no question that staying centered can have a powerful effect on a celebrity's career, but it can also carry over into other areas of life – a phenomenon commonly referred to as the "ripple effect." A focused and grounded approach allowed most highly centered celebrities, 91 percent, to achieve a better sex life (Exhibit 4.4).

EXHIBIT 4.4: *Centeredness = Better Sex*

Highly Centered	Less Centered	Weighted Average
91.4%	82.3%	84.7%

N=1,015 celebrities
(based on 203 entertainment attorneys)

Research shows that a centered approach can yield greater financial success and a better sex life. Anecdotally, we've observed that the benefits of the right mindset can permeate other areas of a person's life – in effect, creating a resounding and positive reverberation.

The rewards of celebrity are great – mansions and private jets, fine timepieces, and vintage champagne – but it's easy to forget that the trappings are the results of much hard work and a suite of unique skills and talents. Success also requires a mindset that fosters perseverance, an unwavering focus, and determination – and the ability to let go of failures and insecurities while embracing victories and strengths.

IMPLICATIONS FOR CELEBRITIES AND THEIR ADVISORS

Acknowledging the need to stay focused is an important step toward doing so – and may be easier to prioritize when the benefits are so easily and clearly quantified. Celebrities that can't do so by themselves should establish the appropriate support network and develop the requisite skills and coping mechanisms. Advisors, on the other hand, can play an instrumental role in helping celebrities to adopt the right mindset and meet their challenges head on. They can also identify the triggers that lead to derailing, provide an objective perspective, and offer assistance in prioritizing and implementing critical duties. Advisors that don't have the background and training to fill this role can partner with another qualified professional to provide the support their clients need.

II

Advanced
PLANNING

ADVANCED
Planning

**AT A
GLANCE**

Significant wealth carries complexity and requires more sophisticated financial strategies to adequately grow or preserve it.

Advanced planning is a suite of cutting-edge services that help wealthy individuals and families structure their assets to be as tax-effective and secure as possible.

The three components of advanced planning – wealth enhancement, estate planning, and asset protection – can be deployed separately or in concert to deliver the right solution for a client.

The goal of wealth enhancement is to help clients create and keep more wealth by leveraging the tax code and regulatory environment.

The estate planning process helps clients structure their assets for distribution after their death and minimize the impact of the associated estate and related taxes.

An individual's assets can be shielded from creditors and litigants with the use of asset protection strategies.

Given the highly customized nature of advanced planning, each solution requires significant thought, detail, and expertise.

There are eight critical and predictive characteristics that every advanced planning strategy should possess to facilitate success.

As discussed in previous chapters, successful celebrities can amass significant wealth. For any individual, great wealth is almost always accompanied by greater complexity, especially on the financial front. We have found that most ultra-affluent individuals have acceptable plans in place to invest their money, and may even have completed some preliminary estate planning. But many neglect the steps needed to most efficaciously enhance, transfer, and protect the wealth they created — a process known as advanced planning. The entertainment attorneys we spoke with believe their celebrity clients are no different and may, in fact, know less about advanced planning expertise and strategies than the average multimillionaire.

So, what is "advanced planning?" Simply put:

Advanced planning is the skillful leveraging of legal, regulatory, and financial expertise to enhance and safeguard an individual's net worth.

It's hard to argue with the objectives and the benefits of advanced planning, and, as a result, it has become a core component of the platform many wealthy individuals and families rely on as part of their comprehensive financial and legal planning processes.

As we'll see, there are a number of ways the opportunities in the tax code and legal system can be used to make your assets work harder. At the same time, it's important to identify the people, organizations, entities, and actions that should be considered in the advanced planning process. For instance:

TAX AUTHORITIES – in short, every government wants its cut, and advanced planning techniques can help minimize tax obligations, ensuring that you pay as little as legally possible.

BUSINESS PARTNERS – whether your business interests are active or passive, majority or minority, harmonious or incompatible, liquid or illiquid, your role and your assets should be clearly defined and addressed. Advanced planning strategies can protect you for future events such as buy-outs, sales, retirement, disability, or death.

LAWSUITS – in an increasingly litigious society, private wealth in often the target of schemers, extended family and disgruntled friends, and business associates. And, if the suits are successful, a fortune can be quickly decimated. Advanced planning offers an intelligent and effective way to structure your assets to discourage lawsuits and provide legal shelter from potential plaintiffs.

Operationally speaking, advanced planning is a critical process that results in the repositioning and restructuring of your assets to preserve and sometimes increase your wealth. For wealthy celebrities the process can be used to maximum effect by leveraging tax laws and regulations, including leading edge tax-driven strategies, and by employing sophisticated financial products in unique ways.

As noted, advanced planning can be conceptualized as involving three interrelated areas: wealth enhancement, estate planning, and asset protection. The following section provides a brief overview of each specialized service.

WEALTH ENHANCEMENT

The idea behind wealth enhancement is to change the nature of an asset so it will be taxed at a lower rate. For instance, income could be transformed into tax-favored dividends, thereby decreasing your overall tax responsibility.

A wide variety of advanced planning strategies exist such as deferred compensation programs or the use of contingent swaps, and related strategies designed to convert ordinary income into capital gains over a specified period of time. Other strategies, such as captive insurance companies, also carry asset protection benefits that may be attractive.

More information translates into more precisely targeted solutions, so if an advanced planner only sees half of your financial equation the results will be proportionate. A seasoned advanced planner with sufficient access to your personal and professional financial affairs can likely deliver a sizeable reduction to your overall tax burden allowing you to keep more of your wealth.

ESTATE PLANNING

As long as there are estate and gift taxes – not to mention the issues surrounding business succession, the need for estate equalization, and the desire of some people to try and control the distribution and use of their wealth from the grave – there will be a need for estate planning. This process helps plan for the future disposition of assets, both current and projected, in accord with an individual's wishes in the most tax-efficient manner. Often the primary goal of estate planning is to mitigate estate taxes, but for many it can be a highly personal and emotional process that calls for rigor, restraint, and careful consideration.

A meaningful part of estate planning for celebrities is being able to dictate to whom and under what conditions their assets will go when they die – as these choices can have a substantial impact on a professional's legacy, reputation, estate, and future earning potential.

Basic estate planning such as revocable trusts and traditional life insurance is sufficient for some clients. Celebrities with more complex financial needs may require a more sophisticated approach which might include self-canceling installment notes, cascading grantor retained annuity trusts, intentionally defective trusts, and remainder purchase marital trusts. In some instances, a combination of structures and strategies are employed to create a highly customized solution such as a dynasty trust funded with life insurance purchased at a 50 percent discount. It's important to remember that estate planning should also address all personal and business assets to ensure the efficient and cost effective transfer of an individual's entire estate.

ASSET PROTECTION

Asset protection is undertaken to safeguard wealth from potential creditors and litigants, including current and former spouses, children, in-laws, family members, and any other people with designs on your money. Its goal is often to deter an adversary and encourage a less-costly compromise. There are numerous strategies to accomplish this objective, but they should all be tailored to your specific situation and needs.

Basic forms of asset protection include liability insurance and dissociation, a process of transferring assets to another person or entity while still retaining access to them. Some examples of dissociation include transferring asset ownership to a spouse or to self-settled spendthrift trusts.

A more sophisticated approach to asset protection involves the use of transformation strategies, a process by which assets are converted into a different structure that is very difficult, if not impossible, for creditors to acquire. The homestead exemption, interests in limited partnerships, and limited liability companies are all examples of transformation strategies. Transformation can also be coupled with monetization and replication, two strategies that often use derivatives.

STATE-OF-THE-ART

Advanced planning is best characterized as either basic or state-of-the-art. The basic form encompasses the plethora of strategies that are readily recognized and generally applicable for all affluent individuals, irrespective of their level of wealth. A good way to demonstrate this is with estate planning. Everyone, regardless of their net worth, should have a will, a durable power of attorney, and so forth. However, the use of intentionally defective trusts or offshore trusts or captive insurance companies or special purpose entities is a step into the state-of-the-art realm.

Skillful application of the basics should be an expectation of any advanced planning process. The basics can accomplish a lot, and for many wealthy clients, a lot is enough. Nonetheless, we find that state-of-the-art strategies are both in high demand and highly appropriate for the majority of our clients based on their preferences and objectives. Moreover, it can be essential to use such select strategies, especially if a client's goals include tax-leveraged growth or conservation of private wealth.

In the past, state-of-the-art strategies came primarily from the universe of private wealth providers such as trust companies, private banks, and tax attorneys. Today, advanced planning specialists have a new role model for designing and implementing money-saving strategies: corporations. Not surprisingly, such strategies can be multifarious given the tax code's complexity. But they are legitimate – also known as *bright line* within the legal community – and effective, the two most important criteria for an advanced planning solution. As a result, corporate tax strategies are playing an increasingly instrumental role in the creation of sophisticated advanced planning strategies for wealth individuals.

THE INNOVATION PROCESS

To better address and deliver creative and powerful solutions for the financial and legal issues facing celebrities today, we rely on "The Innovation Process." We think of it as the cerebral side of advanced planning and, like many strategic initiatives, it starts with an evaluation and concludes with a recommendation. The difference, however, is an unparalleled combination of specialized expertise, extensive probability testing, meticulous case management, and ethical substantiation. In essence, the Innovation Process is comprised of four interconnected activities that ensure state-of-the-art results (Exhibit 5.1):

ENVIRONMENTAL SCANNING entails staying abreast of new and emerging industry trends. It involves an ongoing and systematic evaluation of the evolving legal and regulatory landscape, the changing preferences and requirements of celebrities, and the dynamics at play in the entertainment industry. As part of environmental scanning, we constantly appraise emerging legal strategies and financial products.

SCENARIO THINKING is envisioning where the trends identified during environmental scanning could lead under certain circumstances. Scenarios are hypothetical situations that a celebrity might encounter, as well as the associated probability and risk assessment. As part of the Innovation Process, scenario thinking is used to stress-test new ideas and develop viable advanced planning strategies.

ACTUALIZATION involves turning hypotheses into verifiable strategies backed by actual products. In this process, everything that is needed to bring the idea to life is identified, defined, and assembled. In this stage, we frequently bring in specialists to address a specific component of a plan.

VALIDATION is a multipart process that occurs over time. First and foremost, strategies are validated through a legal and regulatory lens. All concepts must fit, the solution must be appropriate, and the transactions must be legal. We believe that the ethical nature of strategies and tactics is as important as a legal consideration. As such, we take a hard view on whether given techniques not only pass the ethical litmus test, but also make sense for clients and their objectives. Validation also occurs through implementation and through modifications and updates driven by client feedback or changing regulations.

Frequently we find that the Innovation Process yields breakthrough ideas, followed by the methodologies and systems that help those ideas become a plan or a product for a wealthy client. In some ways, the Innovation Process is a search for nuance and relies on in-depth knowledge of the tax code, the ability to reinterpret regulations based on specific client circumstances, and an awareness of the environmental and fiscal conditions needed to maximize each strategy. For celebrities, the process usually takes place behind-the-scenes but it is nonetheless ongoing and a critical part of developing the best possible advanced planning solutions.

EXHIBIT 5.1: *The Innovation Process*

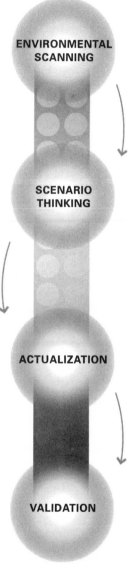

THE CORE ELEMENTS OF ADVANCED PLANNING

To ensure success, there are some additional aspects of advanced planning that must be considered throughout the process. Our experience tells us that strategies are more likely to be effective if they meet the following eight principles:

FLEXIBILITY

DISCRETION

TRANSPARENCY

COHESIVENESS

RISK SENSITIVITY

COST EFFECTIVENESS

EXPLICITNESS

LEGITIMACY

These eight qualities work together and should be treated as prerequisites in any affluent client case. In fact, the competency exhibited by leading advanced planners is directly related to their understanding and execution of these eight core elements.

FLEXIBILITY: Advanced planning must be able to change and adapt to a celebrity's evolving circumstances or shifting financial and legal environments. Successful advanced planners are flexible, accommodating, well informed, and capable of quickly identifying and analyzing a range of anticipated scenarios.

DISCRETION: A high degree of discretion is required of any advisor working with extremely wealthy individuals, especially those with public careers and lives. As it relates to advanced planning, discretion regarding specific strategies can help avoid unwanted attention, unnecessary levels of questioning, and retroactive rule changes. Prudence should also be used when it comes to the nature and details of the interpersonal relationship between the advanced planner and the client. High-quality advanced planners always presume that all communications – written or verbal, formal or informal – could later be examined and act accordingly.

TRANSPARENCY: Public discussions on the intricacies of a sophisticated or customized advanced planning strategy can lead to inappropriate applications or improper execution. Nonetheless, it is important for each strategy to be as transparent as possible and available to scrutiny by authorities.

COHESIVENESS: While the components of advanced planning can be employed on a standalone basis, a shared philosophy and a certain degree of integration should inform all such planning. This will help ensure that the client's objectives remain the focus of all efforts and allow strategies to work in more than one capacity, if possible. Experienced advanced planners can capture additional value for clients by looking across the three different areas of advanced planning to identify synergies.

RISK SENSITIVITY: As noted previously, the spectrum of advanced planning strategies spans from the plain vanilla to the truly esoteric. Without stepping over any legal boundaries, there is still ample room to be aggressive. Not surprisingly, many of the most innovative and state-of-the-art advanced planning strategies tend to be more aggressive. It is therefore critical that celebrities and their other advisors understand the level of aggressiveness associated with a particular strategy and consider it in the context of their risk tolerance.

COST EFFECTIVENESS: There are times when being on the cutting edge carries too high a price tag for the result. Other times, more mainstream solutions are sufficient. Advanced planners must work with their celebrity clients to balance the benefits of a recommended course of action with both its financial and psychological costs.

EXPLICITNESS: Some celebrities want simple and readily understood solutions to their financial and legal issues. Others rely more heavily on their team of advisors to find the best solutions for them. At the same time, there are some who enjoy the details and intricacies of a strategy or product. We advocate that all clients – no matter their level of interest or savvy – understand the essence, if not the details, of the advanced planning strategies they will implement. We therefore bear the responsibility of communicating with celebrities and their other advisors in a way that suits their personal style and allows them to make informed decisions.

LEGITIMACY: Advanced planning should never incorporate strategies or techniques that are – or may be perceived as – illegal or unethical. Considering how much can be accomplished by operating squarely within the law, it is simply greed, ego or sheer stupidity that leads celebrities and advisors to cross the line. Greater scrutiny can be expected from both domestic and international authorities on these types of activities and it is not worth inviting further attention with questionable transactions.

IMPLICATIONS FOR CELEBRITIES AND THEIR ADVISORS

In the world of significant wealth, a comprehensive financial plan must be broader than an investment policy, for instance, and should incorporate strategies that preserve and enhance wealth and help individuals extract the greatest benefit from current tax regulations. Advanced planning specialists are the professionals who have the expertise and the experience to design and deliver solutions that enable celebrities to structure their wealth in ways that suit their objectives and priorities, while retaining as much of it as possible.

To get the best result, a celebrity must be sufficiently involved in the process to clarify his or her goals, provide the access and information an advanced planner needs, and take the time to understand the recommended plan. An advisor must recognize that advanced planning can deliver highly-valued results to wealthy clients and may be an essential part of a balanced financial program. Cultivating relationships with advanced planners helps broaden the network and capabilities of most advisors and positions them to work more effectively with affluent clients.

6

WEALTH
Enhancement

AT A GLANCE

Wealth enhancement is a specialized discipline that helps wealthy individuals transform the nature of certain assets, often using tax-advantaged structures, consequently reducing or eliminating the tax obligation associated with the asset in its original form.

Wealth enhancement can be accomplished in a number of ways using a combination of legal transactions, legal structures, and financial products.

Most celebrities want to pay less in taxes but have not taken any steps or actions to do so, largely because the capability was never presented to them.

Most celebrities would be interested in exploring the application, and impact, of wealth enhancement planning to their current tax scenarios.

Wealth enhancement solutions are complicated, often esoteric, and designed specifically to work within the context of an individual's personal and financial affairs while addressing a specific goal.

Paying less in taxes is appealing to almost everyone, especially the wealthy. And all of our clients — celebrities included — have indicated an interest in decreasing their current tax burden, including income, estate, and capital gains taxes. It is for these reasons that wealth enhancement strategies can be an effective addition to an affluent individual's overall financial plan.

So, what is "wealth enhancement?" Simply put:

The process of wealth enhancement uses legal transactions, legal structures, and financial products to convert the character of revenues and assets to mitigate select taxes.

In many respects, the objective of wealth enhancement is to convert revenue streams taxed at one rate to revenues streams that will be taxed at a lower rate. These strategies may also entail using losses to offset gains.

CELEBRITIES AND WEALTH ENHANCEMENT

Like other high-net-worth individuals, wealthy celebrities are extremely receptive to reducing the amount of money they pay in taxes; nearly all are interested in doing so (Exhibit 6.1).

EXHIBIT 6.1: *Very or Extremely Interested in Ways to Restructure and Lower Their Taxes*

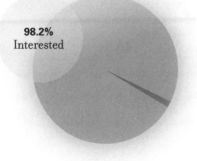

98.2%
Interested

N=1,015 celebrities
(based on 203 entertainment attorneys)

Despite their acute interest, few celebrities have taken steps to leverage their sources of income in ways that will allow them to mitigate taxes. In fact, only one in five celebrities have done so, though status-oriented celebs were twice as likely as craft-oriented celebs to have already pursued this course of action (Exhibit 6.2).

EXHIBIT 6.2: *Have Leveraged Their Entertainment Businesses and/or Ongoing Revenue Streams to Enhance Their Wealth*

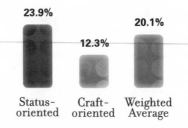

23.9%

12.3%

20.1%

Status-oriented   Craft-oriented   Weighted Average

N=1,015 celebrities
(based on 203 entertainment attorneys)

Given the significant gap between the number of celebrities who want to reduce their taxes and the number who had actually implemented tax-reduction strategies, we wanted to know why so few of them had taken action. Far and away, the main reason most celebs had not yet acted was because they'd never worked with a professional who possessed the requisite expertise. Many of them realized that a number of sophisticated tax strategies existed, requiring a specific proficiency to be correctly developed and implemented. About 90 percent of celebs did not have a resource to provide them recommendations or insights on wealth enhancement (Exhibit 6.3). Even so, just one in ten celebrities are determined by the complicated nature of these strategies as a barrier and only one percent felt they might be illegal or unethical.

EXHIBIT 6.3: *Reasons for Not Taking Steps to Enhance Wealth*

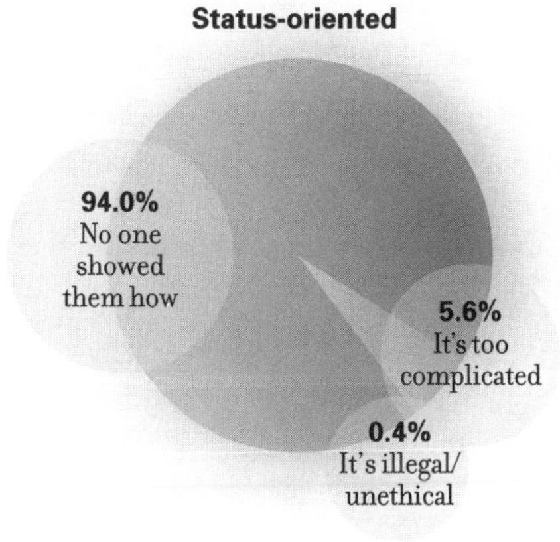

Status-oriented

94.0%
No one
showed
them how

5.6%
It's too
complicated

0.4%
It's illegal/
unethical

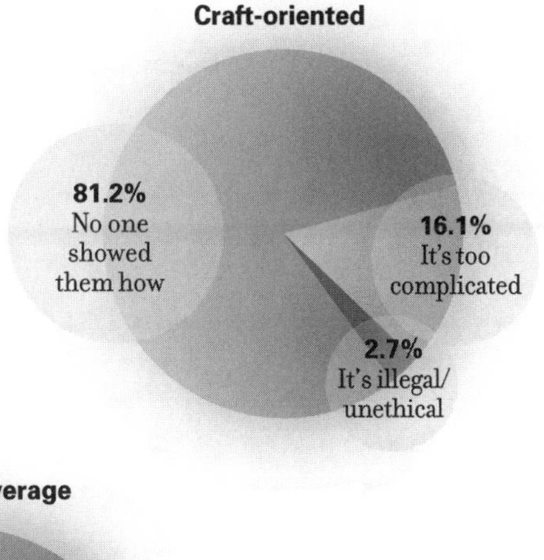

Craft-oriented

81.2%
No one
showed
them how

16.1%
It's too
complicated

2.7%
It's illegal/
unethical

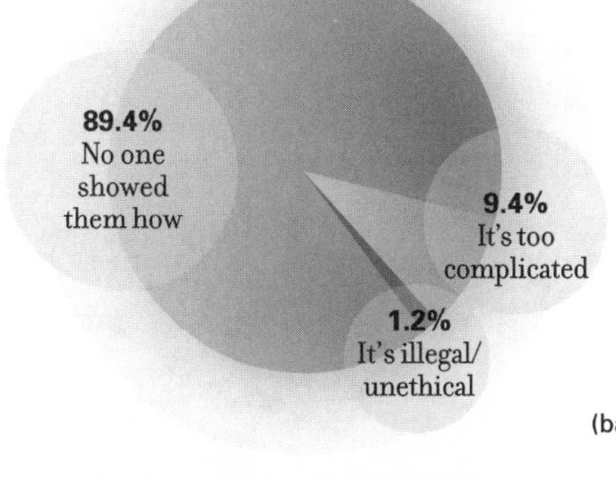

Weighted Average

89.4%
No one
showed
them how

9.4%
It's too
complicated

1.2%
It's illegal/
unethical

N=811 celebrities
(based on 203 entertainment attorneys)

These results indicate that the celebrity population has likely been underserved when it comes to wealth enhancement and have financial situations that would be fertile ground for advisors who want to help celebrities enhance their wealth.

Case Studies

We have always found that the best way to help our clients understand the possibilities of advanced planning is through case studies. It's important to remember that no two cases are alike, but certain philosophies and approaches can be leveraged in pursuit of similar goals. The three examples of wealth enhancement solutions outlined below require a very specific set of circumstances, but provide a clear sense of each celebrity client's issues and goals, the appropriateness of actions that were taken, and the results.

Actor

NOW PLAYING

TAX-ADVANTAGED SELF-PROVIDED LOANS

SCENARIO An actor with a net worth in excess of US$50 million and an annual income of approximately US$5 million, much of which comes from royalties and participation arrangements, wants to lower his income tax bill.

1. Several years ago we established a loan-out corporation for the actor in a non-US domicile known for its favorable tax treaties.

2. We developed a deferred compensation program within his loan-out corporation and directed his non-US royalties and participations into the program.

3. The assets in the deferred compensation program were invested in cash and cash-equivalents to ensure safety of principal.

RESULT With this structure, the loan-out corporation can make loans that are interest- and principal-deferred after one year and one day have passed. Loans were made to the actor using the assets in the deferred compensation program as funding; no current taxes were owed on the loans. This solution allows the actor to access his current earnings while decreasing his current tax obligations.

Composer

HEDGING A CATALOG

SCENARIO A composer and her husband of 21-years were recently divorced and she owes him a significant lump sum settlement. Her goal is to retain ownership of her song catalog, as it is her largest and most valuable asset, while meeting the terms of the judgment.

1. We designed a derivative transaction to "convert" the catalog into a security.

2. We hedged the security to create liquidity and invested 80 percent of the security's total value – in this case, US$24 million – in a structured note based on a basket of hedge funds and private companies.

3. The investment was leveraged up three times, increasing its total value to US$72 million.

4. We used a loan taken against the structured note, at LIBOR + 20 basis points, to zero out the investment profits on an annual basis.

5. A portion of the loan is used to satisfy the composer's obligation in her divorce settlement and pay off the loan; she will retain any residual profits.

RESULT In five years we will unwind the structured note, at which time the ex-husband will have been paid in total, the composer will realize US$2.2 million in profit, and she will have complete ownership of her catalog.

Musician

RIGHTS ACQUISITIONS

SCENARIO A musician wants to invest in other artists' properties that she believes will have long-term popularity by purchasing royalty streams. Her goal is to increase her income without adding to her current tax burden.

1. We establish a trust within a partnership structure; the trust will own any acquisitions.

2. The trust is funded using pre-tax income from the musician's own royalty stream.

3. The musician uses the assets in the trust to purchase the rights to individual songs by other artists.

4. In two instances we packaged a selection of songs, converted them into derivatives, and leveraged them up. This transaction enabled the trustee to sell a portion of the revenue streams from the packages for a specified period of time, after which the revenue reverted to the musician.

5. The proceeds from the sales were used to purchase additional songs on a tax-advantaged basis and interest deductions were used to offset other income.

RESULT The rights acquisitions have helped the musician create a meaningful and growing asset that generates a consistent stream of income, increasing her overall net worth. The trust allows her to own the rights and receive the income without any immediate tax implications. When she eventually takes profits from the partnership, they will be taxed as capital gains not ordinary income.

IMPLICATIONS FOR CELEBRITIES AND THEIR ADVISORS

A number of creative approaches can be taken to reduce the current tax responsibilities of wealthy celebrities, but few have explored their options. Celebrities who want to investigate the application of wealth enhancement to their financial situations should work with their team of advisors to clarify their goals and priorities. At the same time, advisors should be aware that there is a high degree of interest among wealthy celebrities to learn more about wealth enhancement. They should make the effort to acquire some base knowledge about the discipline, cultivate working relationships with advanced planners who can help identify opportunities and develop the appropriate strategies, and be proactive in finding and presenting solutions to their clients.

7 ESTATE *Planning*

Estate planning is a multi-faceted service that enables wealthy individuals to designate exactly how their assets will be distributed upon their death. Additionally, many estate planning techniques and strategies use structures and transactions that mitigate taxes and help increase wealth while the client is still alive.

Nearly all celebrities want to provide for their families and loved ones after their death and a high percentage of them already have estate plans.

The estate plans of most celebrities who do have them are seriously outdated – either due to a milestone event in their life, a marked increase in wealth, or changing tax laws – and need to be revisited and revised.

Those that don't have estate plans are either uncomfortable dealing with the highly emotional and complex issues that arise during the process or they haven't yet carved out the time to devote to the initiative.

Like wealth enhancement, estate planning solutions are complicated, often esoteric, and designed specifically to work within the context of an individual's personal and financial affairs to address specific estate planning goals.

At some level,

nearly everyone is a candidate for estate planning. In particular, it can help the wealthy individuals that want:

To ensure that their families and loved ones are provided for adequately after their death.

To avoid the involvement of state or federal governments in the distribution of their estates.

To dictate how and to whom their assets will be distributed after their death.

To ensure that the maximum amount possible is transferred to their loved ones while paying the minimum amount of taxes.

To be philanthropic and capture the tax advantages associated with charitable donations.

To plan adequately for the estate tax while preserving the estate's value.

People with a seven-figure net worth should, at a minimum, engage in basic estate planning – and for those with greater wealth, it is a necessity. However, basic estate planning is sometimes insufficient for most affluent celebrities as their assets, relationships, and goals are often complicated and unique. As a result, many celebrities turn to advanced planners to access the more sophisticated techniques that will enable them to accomplish their estate planning goals.

So, what is "estate planning?" Simply put:

Estate planning is the process of legally structuring the future disposition of current and projected assets.

Every estate plan includes documents that designate how your assets will be disposed at death, such as a will. Estate planning can, however, involve much more. Lifetime giving – annual gifts to relatives and non-profit organizations or private foundations and trusts that are overseen by a board and managed to your specifications, for example – is one possible facet of estate planning. Another is the exclusion of assets, an effort to reduce the overall size of your estate and, in turn, reduce the amount of the estate tax that will be owed. For instance, life insurance can be excluded from a taxable estate with the use of properly structured trusts. Another strategy allows the value of an asset, such as the equity stake in a business, to be "frozen" at its current level allowing any subsequent appreciation to be free of estate tax.

CELEBRITIES AND ESTATE PLANNING

It's no surprise that most wealthy celebrities want to provide for the people who are most important to them when they die. This is a concern for almost 90 percent of status-oriented celebs and nearly all of the craft-oriented celebs (Exhibit 7.1).

EXHIBIT 7.1: *Concerned With the Well-being of Loved Ones*

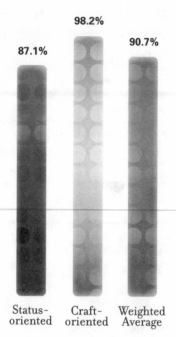

87.1%
98.2%
90.7%

Status-oriented   Craft-oriented   Weighted Average

N=1,015 celebrities
(based on 203 entertainment attorneys)

And, logically, most celebrities had an estate plan that allowed them to provide for their loved ones. About three-quarters of status-oriented entertainers and slightly more, 87 percent, of craft-oriented professionals had put the time, thought, and effort into creating a plan (Exhibit 7.2). However, as we shall see, a number of those estate plans are outdated.

EXHIBIT 7.2: *Have an Estate Plan*

Status-oriented: 74.8%
Craft-oriented: 86.8%
Weighted Average: 78.7%

N=1,015 celebrities
(based on 203 entertainment attorneys)

Given the sizeable wealth of the celebrities in our study, we wanted to understand why a portion of them did not have an estate plan. We used a factor analytic technique to identify the principal reasons they did not have one, and some major differences in our segments were revealed (Exhibit 7.3).

Death, especially one's own mortality, can be a difficult topic to deal with, and this is the case for 71 percent of status-oriented celebs without an estate plan. The emotional strain is too great, and avoidance is often the easiest course of action. Craft-oriented professionals, by contrast, felt differently. Estate planning is a problematic subject for just 19 percent of them, indicating a willingness to face the issues that accompany estate planning as a means to an end.

When it comes to time, however, an overbooked calendar was the reason just 23 percent of status-oriented celebrities and 76 percent of their craft-oriented counterparts had not focused on estate planning. They knew it would be a good idea, but they just could not seem to fit it in with the other activities they had planned.

The remaining celebrities, just 6 percent, believed that they did not have a need for an estate plan. The reasons for this vary — such as naming spouses as the sole beneficiary or a lack of heirs — but the decision may leave a large estate in the hands of a civil servant. If a celebrity wants a say in how his or her wealth will be distributed upon their death, then an estate plan is required.

EXHIBIT 7.3: *Why No Estate Plan*

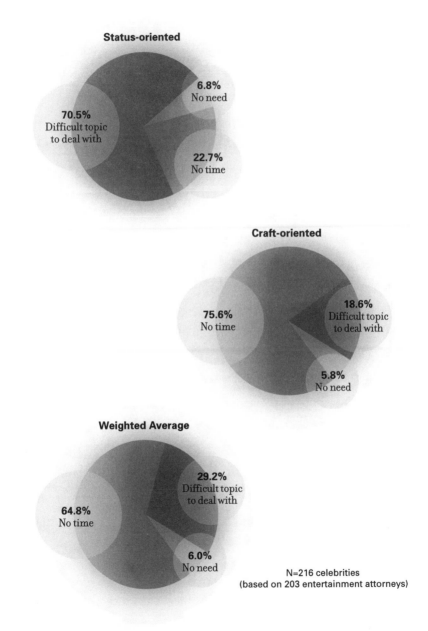

Status-oriented

6.8%
No need

70.5%
Difficult topic
to deal with

22.7%
No time

Craft-oriented

75.6%
No time

18.6%
Difficult topic
to deal with

5.8%
No need

Weighted Average

29.2%
Difficult topic
to deal with

64.8%
No time

6.0%
No need

N=216 celebrities
(based on 203 entertainment attorneys)

Although the majority of celebrities did have an estate plan, many were woefully outdated and likely to no longer reflect the assets, circumstances, and desires of the individual for whom it was drafted. More than half of the celebs, 53 percent, had a plan that was more than six years old — stale, according to a group of private client attorneys we consulted (Exhibit 7.4). Another 35 percent had a plan that was between three and six years old, and only 13 percent had completed a plan at some point within the previous three years.

EXHIBIT 7.4: *Age of Estate Plans*

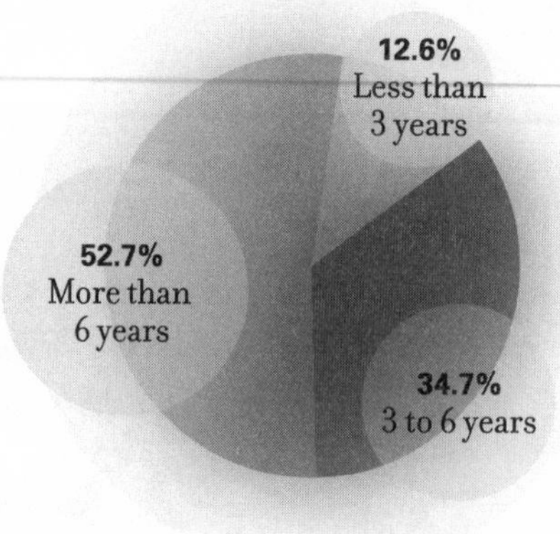

12.6%
Less than
3 years

52.7%
More than
6 years

34.7%
3 to 6 years

N=799 celebrities
(based on 203 entertainment attorneys)

Indeed, most tax and estate attorneys agree that two to three years is the point after which an estate plan should be revisited. No matter how well conceived and implemented an estate plan is, if the tax codes change it can have a devastating effect on the effort — and the tax code is in a near perpetual state of flux.

Of course, it's not just the regulatory environment that can date an estate plan; changes in a client's life have the same effect. A whopping 93 percent of celebrities are wealthier now then when they had their most recent estate plan prepared (Exhibit 7.5), meaning a portion of their assets is almost certainly not addressed.

EXHIBIT 7.5: *Wealthier Since the Estate Plan*

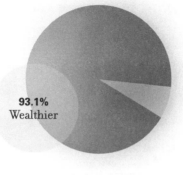

93.1%
Wealthier

N=1,015 celebrities
(based on 203 entertainment attorneys)

Similarly, landmark events can impact the effectiveness and accuracy of a plan. About two-thirds of celebrities had experienced such an event – perhaps a marriage or divorce, the birth of a child or grandchild, a death in the family – and had not yet updated their plans to reflect their current situation (Exhibit 7.6).

EXHIBIT 7.6: *Experienced a Life-Changing Event Since the Estate Plan*

64.3%
Life-changing
event

N=799 celebrities
(based on 203 entertainment attorneys)

In sum, while most celebrities do indeed have estate plans, it's probable that they're out of date. Compounding the problem is the fact that new strategies have been developed — are being developed every day — that are far more advanced and effective than older methods. As a result, many celebrities may be missing out on an opportunity to more efficiently preserve their wealth for future generations. Regardless of the reasons, a plan that has not been updated is unlikely to accomplish a celebrity's current goals and objectives.

Case Studies

As mentioned previously, we have always found case studies to be a useful tool in demonstrating the potential of advanced planning to our clients. It's important to remember that no two cases are alike, but certain philosophies and approaches can be leveraged in pursuit of similar goals. The three examples of estate planning solutions outlined below require a very specific set of circumstances, but provide a clear sense of each client's issues and goals, the actions that were taken, and the actual or anticipated results.

Supermodel

FREEZING AND TRANSFERRING BUSINESS INTERESTS

SCENARIO Over the course of her career, a supermodel used her earnings to diversify her portfolio in anticipation of an early retirement. She invested in more than 35 businesses outside the media and entertainment sector, many of which tripled and quadrupled in value. Expectations remain high for continued growth and she wants to shield any future appreciation from estate taxes.

1. We worked with a valuation specialist to appraise the model's equity and determine a value.

2. We used a derivative transaction to transfer the business interests – worth US$28 million – into an intentionally defective grantor trust, thereby postponing the payment of taxes for 20 years.

3. We facilitated loans for the model's business partners through special purpose entities, which were used to buy the revenue streams generated from the model's ownership stake at net present value from the trust.

4. The liquid assets in the trust, including all future appreciation, were used as collateral for a floating, non-recourse credit line for the model's family members. The size of the credit line is a function of business profits.

RESULT The growth of the model's business interests, projected to increase 6 percent annually to more than US$100 million, will not be subject to estate taxes. Her obligation will be limited to the taxes due on the "frozen" value.

T.V. Personality

MULTIPLE CHARITABLE STRUCTURES

SCENARIO A TV personality wants to support causes that provide housing, food, education, and medical care to needy children. The substantial tax deduction from an outright contribution is attractive, but he doesn't want to cede total control of his assets since he will have ongoing income needs and hopes to provide generously for his own children after his death.

1. We reviewed the entertainer's assets to determine those most suitable to fund planned gifts.

2. We established a private foundation for him and funded it with US$10 million in low-basis stock, creating an immediate tax deduction.

3. We then established an increasing charitable lead trust and funded it with some of his participation interests with a value of US$14 million.

4. Next we established a charitable remainder trust with a 20-year term using US$9 million in commercial real estate owned by the entertainer.

RESULT   The charitable lead trust and charitable remainder trust will work together to provide the entertainer with an annual income of US$850,000 for the next 20 years and a projected US$39 million will pass to his children – free of estate taxes – upon his death. His private foundation will have an endowment of US$86 million in 20 years and will be overseen by his children, ensuring that the charities of greatest interest to him will continue to prosper.

Film Producer

LIFE INSURANCE AT A DISCOUNT

SCENARIO   A film producer needs US$40 million in life insurance but is balking at the quoted premiums and doesn't want the value of the policy to increase his estate and the associated tax obligation.

1. We established an irrevocable life insurance trust so the value and proceeds of the policy are outside of the producer's estate.

2. We hedged the producer's US$12 million single-stock holding, investing the proceeds in a hedge fund derivative that uses a warrant structure.

3. The producer took a loan against the derivative at LIBOR + 80 basis points and used a split-dollar arrangement to pay for the life insurance.

RESULT The life insurance will be paid-up in seven years at approximately half the cost of paying for it on an out-of-pocket basis. The producer will have the coverage he needs without negatively impacting his estate, and may profit from the investment returns.

IMPLICATIONS FOR CELEBRITIES AND THEIR ADVISORS

For many individuals — even some that have significant assets to protect — estate planning remains an outstanding component of their overall financial plan, and by leaving it unresolved they place their assets and their beneficiaries at risk. Fortunately, the universe of affluent celebrities has embraced estate planning and acknowledged its importance in a well-managed, long-term wealth management solution. In fact, more celebrities than many other high-net-worth segments have plans; as a point of comparison, just 59 percent of similarly wealthy hedge fund professionals have estate plans.

The issue at stake for celebrities is the quality and accuracy of their plans. By and large, the majority of plans we see are sorely outdated and no longer function as intended. Effective estate planning is, in essence, a continuum. Both celebrities and their advisors must commit to the ongoing nature of the process. Advanced planners must periodically evaluate estate planning documents and strategies against the current regulatory environment and each client's state of affairs. Doing so will ensure that the settlement of an estate is handled exactly as its owner specified.

ASSET
Protection

AT A GLANCE

Despite the public's love affair with celebrities, many are the target of unwanted attention and baseless lawsuits.

Asset protection is a component of advanced planning that helps celebrities structure their wealth in ways that deter gold diggers, business creditors, disillusioned ex-spouses, jilted lovers, unhappy investors, and the like.

Regrettably, many celebrities know from experience that facing a lawsuit without completing any asset protection planning can be costly and painful.

Most celebrities will face more legal problems down the road and, as such, are interested in exploring the ways asset protection can help them prepare and preserve their wealth.

Asset protection must be approached as part of an overall financial plan and all strategies must be morally and economically sound in order to pass legal inspection.

Asset protection can be accomplished in a number of ways but, like other components of advanced planning, it is unique to the owner of the assets and his or her surrounding circumstances.

In an ideal world, everyone would be prepared for unexpected events and disasters. But you don't have to be a pessimist to plan for the worst. It's possible to manage risks in ways that will protect you and your assets from unwanted attention and unfounded legal action. The key is to do it in a timely and effective fashion that has little to no downside — and that's the role that asset protection can play.

While asset protection is a discrete form of legal planning, it is derivative of other disciplines such as risk management. The goal is to provide you and your assets with a viable defense against litigants and creditors. Given the increasingly litigious nature of society and the pervasive belief that all celebrities are super-rich, asset protection is a wise move for most—if not all—wealthy celebs.

So, what is "asset protection?" Simply put:

Asset protection planning is the process of employing risk management products and legally acceptable strategies to ensure a person's wealth is not unjustly taken from him or her.

The preferred course of action – for most people – is to avoid litigation. The best asset protection plans are never even tested in court; after reviewing the way assets have been structured, creditors and litigants conclude that going to court would be too costly and difficult, and they choose to settle. Those cases that do make it to trial often result in small or unpaid judgments, as the assets are simply and legitimately not accessible.

Critical to successful asset protection planning is timing. By and large, you have to implement strategies that would effectively protect your wealth before problems arise. In essence, it's a form of pre-litigation planning. While certain circumstances permit celebrities to use asset protection strategies after the fact, they are relatively few and far between.

THE COURT'S PERSPECTIVE

Not surprisingly, judges and juries tend to frown on wealthy and successful people that try to avoid paying their debts. As such, the transactions and structures that protect the wealth of high-profile individuals, from creditors should make economic sense within the context of an overall financial plan. This means that asset protection planning, to the extent possible, should happen in conjunction with, or as an offshoot of, other legal planning efforts. Not only is this a logical approach from a financial perspective, it provides a built-in rationale for each action should those actions come under scrutiny.

Successful asset protection planning must justify the way wealth is organized and the manner in which assets were transferred into various legal structures such as trusts, partnerships, and corporate entities. The advanced planner must be capable of presenting the facts surrounding the implementation of asset protection strategies in a way that will resonate with a judge or jury and demonstrate that:

> The celebrity was morally right in his or her actions.

> The strategies implemented were economically and legally sound given the celebrity's personal, professional, and financial situation.

CELEBRITIES AND ASSET PROTECTION PLANNING

Like most wealthy individuals, celebrities focus on protecting their assets only after they have had their fortunes risked or lost. Unfortunately, that is often too late. The time to prepare for unjust legal actions is before they occur.

As it turns out, more than half of celebrities in the study sample had already been involved in unjust lawsuits or divorce proceedings (Exhibit 8.1). This figure is much higher than it is for the rest of the wealthy population, likely due to the high-profile of celebrities and the warped public perception of celebrity wealth. It's frightening how quickly a lawsuit can materialize when people think you're amazingly wealthy.

The disparity between segments tells another story, however. Status-oriented celebs were more than three times as likely to have been involved in a nasty legal matter than craft-oriented celebs — a byproduct of their lifestyle and personal relationships.

EXHIBIT 8.1: *Been Involved in Unjust Lawsuits and/or Divorce Proceedings*

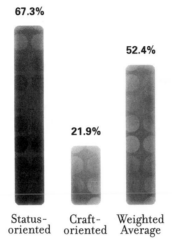

67.3%

52.4%

21.9%

Status-   Craft-   Weighted
oriented   oriented   Average

N=1,015 celebrities
(based on 203 entertainment attorneys)

Clearly, the bad memories have lingered as most celebrities were concerned about future involvement in similar cases. Nearly 90 percent of status-oriented celebs and 78 percent of craft-oriented celebs were anxious about being targeted further (Exhibit 8.2). After all, an unfavorable legal decision or a messy divorce can decimate years of wealth creation.

And most celebrities have an overwhelming, but often unvoiced, fear that a judge and jury will have a bias against them due to their wealth and assume they can easily afford losses.

EXHIBIT 8.2: *Concerned About Being Involved in Unjust Lawsuits and/or Divorce Proceedings*

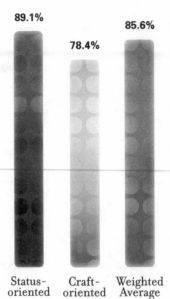

89.1%

78.4%

85.6%

Status-oriented   Craft-oriented   Weighted Average

N=1,015 celebrities
(based on 203 entertainment attorneys)

For wealthy celebrities, we found that asset protection planning carries the same sense of urgency as its advanced planning counterparts — wealth enhancement planning and estate planning. Even though most celebs find the idea of a smaller tax bill appealing, very few had engaged in proper wealth enhancement activities. And while a similarly large number of celebrities wanted to control the disposition of their estate, very few had up-to-date estate plans. Sadly, there is very little difference when it comes to asset protection despite significant experience with, or knowledge of, unfounded lawsuits: Even though 86 percent of celebrities feared future lawsuits, only 28 percent had taken the steps to protect their assets (Exhibit 8.3).

EXHIBIT 8.3: *Have an Asset Protection Plan*

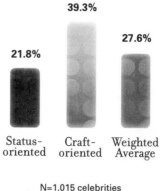

39.3%

27.6%

21.8%

Status-   Craft-   Weighted
oriented   oriented   Average

N=1,015 celebrities
(based on 203 entertainment attorneys)

As in our analysis of the celebs without a current estate plan, we used factor analysis to identify the principal motivation for their not having an asset protection plan. By and large, the main reason most celebs didn't have plans was because no one with the expertise had introduced the topic and shown them how. Complexity is a deterrent to asset protection for a much smaller group, dominated by craft-oriented celebs, and a relative handful were unsure about the legality of such planning or felt they had no need to protect their wealth (Exhibit 8.4).

EXHIBIT 8.4: *Why No Asset Protection Plan*

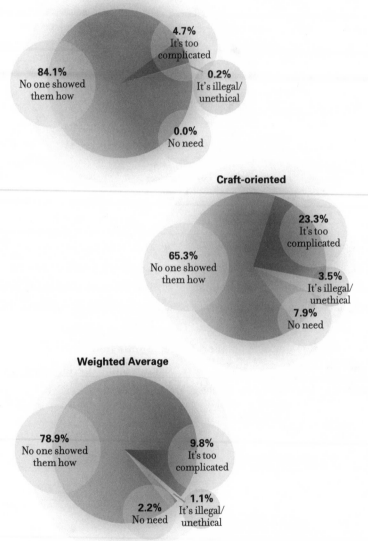

Status-oriented

4.7%
It's too complicated

84.1%
No one showed them how

0.2%
It's illegal/ unethical

0.0%
No need

Craft-oriented

23.3%
It's too complicated

65.3%
No one showed them how

3.5%
It's illegal/ unethical

7.9%
No need

Weighted Average

78.9%
No one showed them how

9.8%
It's too complicated

2.2%
No need

1.1%
It's illegal/ unethical

N=667 celebrities
(based on 203 entertainment attorneys)

Case Studies

As noted in the previous two chapters, we often rely on case studies to help our clients understand the power and potential of advanced planning. Again, it's important to remember that no two cases are alike, but certain philosophies and approaches can be leveraged in the pursuit of similar goals. The three examples of asset protection solutions outlined below are highly customized and must include an arm's length relationship between the various parties involved to be successful. Each requires a very specific set of circumstances, but each provides a clear sense of each client's issues and goals, the actions that were taken, and the actual or anticipated results.

Actor

EQUITY STRIPPING

SCENARIO To deter frivolous lawsuits, a renowned actor wanted to diminish the value of his personal holdings to be less appealing to potential litigants.

1. We established a series of trusts to hold the actor's personal and commercial real estate, private jet, yacht, and collections of fine art, jewelry, and watches valued at US$61 million.

2. We arranged for the appraisal of his assets and then obtained loans against the property for their full value through a commercial bank.

3. We created another trust to invest the assets from the loans in a hedge fund and named someone else the beneficiary on the trust, further dissociating the actor from the assets.

If the hedge fund outperforms the loan rate, the actor will make money while his assets are protected from creditors and litigants.

4. The bank, in turn, sold a promissory note for the loans to a second hedge fund. Creditors will be able to identify the bank, but not the hedge fund, creating another layer of anonymity for the actor. The structures will remain in place until he is in a position to unwind them.

RESULT Securing loans against the actor's property effectively "strips" the equity from his assets, leaving them encumbered and no longer an attractive target.

Pop Band

PROTECTING WEALTH & GENERATING REVENUE

SCENARIO A popular band was planning an open-ended world tour. The amount of liability coverage they could access through conventional means was considered insufficient by the band members and their management team; everyone was concerned about placing themselves and their assets at risk.

1. We formed an offshore captive insurance company and funded it with US$8.6 million of the band's money.

2. Through the captive, the appropriate amount of traditional liability insurance was purchased for the band at a cost of US$3 million.

3. We placed the remaining US$5.6 million, a reserve for claims and settlements, in a principal protected structured note to minimize the risk of underperformance.

4. The assets in the note were leveraged up four times, allowing a total of US$22.4 million to work as an investment.

RESULT   The tour ended after 30 months with no mishaps or legal action and the captive insurance company was dissolved. The investment had generated an additional US$2.8 million, which was distributed to the band members.

Entertainers

FLOATING ISLANDS

SCENARIO   A number of unaffiliated entertainers – each with a history of lawsuits – were seeking ways to further protect themselves.

1. We established a series of self-settled trusts in select jurisdictions around the world.

2. The group of participants was identified and we worked with each entertainer to liquidate a specified portion of their assets.

3. The assets were distributed across the trusts and a set of algorithms tied to exchange rates was used to control the ongoing movement of assets between trusts.

4. Our existing relationships with local fiduciaries will provide access to the assets, if needed.

RESULT   Money in movement is difficult to find and quantify, which can help shield the entertainers and their assets from unsubstantiated legal action. Participants are able to withdraw their assets at any time without disrupting the collective effort, which will continue as long as deemed necessary.

IMPLICATIONS FOR CELEBRITIES AND THEIR ADVISORS

Protecting a fortune can be an important and emotional issue for many, especially those that live their lives in the spotlight and are under constant appraisal by opportunists. Most celebrities are familiar with groundless claims and costly legal proceedings, but very few have taken the steps to prepare themselves for future onslaughts. Celebrities should express their concerns and their assets protection goals to their closest advisors, so the right expertise can be brought in to craft and deliver solutions.

Advisors must familiarize themselves with the techniques and structures that enable asset protection, how each can function as part of an overarching financial program, and the legal criteria that must be met in order to be deemed effective in a court of law. Finally, having a strong network of advanced planning specialists will allow for responsiveness and action when it is needed most.

III

Making it
work

THE
Virtuous Cycle

AT A GLANCE

The Virtuous Cycle is the process advanced planners use to best serve their affluent clients.

The Virtuous Cycle structures the interaction between the client and the advanced planner to maximum effect, while providing an ethical framework that ensures the celebrity client's needs and interests are optimized at all times.

From an operational standpoint, the Virtuous Cycle consists of six successive phases that build on one another, helping to initiate, advance, and conclude the process.

Experienced advanced planners acknowledge the dynamic nature of their field and treat the Virtuous Cycle as a continuous process, allowing them to accommodate the shifts in a client's needs and circumstances.

The Virtuous Cycle

is the process used by advanced planners to identify, design, and deliver the best solutions for their wealthy clients. The name reflects the characteristics that set it — and the professionals that rely on it — apart from other methods and the competition.

Virtue represents the ethical approach and high standards taken by advanced planners, and *Cycle* refers to the multiple steps needed to complete the process.

The Virtuous Cycle is a best-in-class model that encompasses years of quantitative analysis of the behaviors and actions used by respected financial and legal experts with their affluent clients – including celebrities. It was developed scientifically, in the statistical laboratory, and practically, through its continued use by elite advisors. It has been modified based on feedback from practitioners, benchmarked using quality process analysis, and validated through thousands of cross-sectional debriefings.

One expert in the advanced planning field defined the Virtuous Cycle as, "An alchemic process where leading-edge financial and legal advisors use wisdom to broker the identification of solutions to problems and deliver strategies that resolve the issues." Though flowery, his definition captures several key elements of the process: the wisdom of advisors, solutions to problems, and the delivery of strategies.

Operationally, the Virtuous Cycle consists of the phases a celebrity and an advanced planner would move through together to identify and employ the proper strategies. At the same time, involvement and collaboration among the various advisors, specialists, and the client is the foundation of a successful effort. Like many systematic approaches, the Virtuous Cycle is only as effective as the individuals and information involved. So, if a tax code is interpreted incorrectly or financial data is inaccurate, the results may be flawed despite strict adherence to the process.

THE PHASES OF THE VIRTUOUS CYCLE

The Virtuous Cycle is comprised of six distinct phases (Exhibit 9.1). Although we present the process as sequential, we often find that it must be adapted to each client situation. Continuous feedback from clients and other advisors is a meaningful part of the process and may result in some backtracking, revisions, and adjustments to ensure the best results. In short, it is a process that is most effective when it remains dynamic and fluid.

The phases of the process are:

PROFILING

NETWORKING

RECOMMENDATIONS

IMPLEMENTATION

RESULTS

FOLLOW-THROUGH

EXHIBIT 9.1: *The Virtuous Cycle*

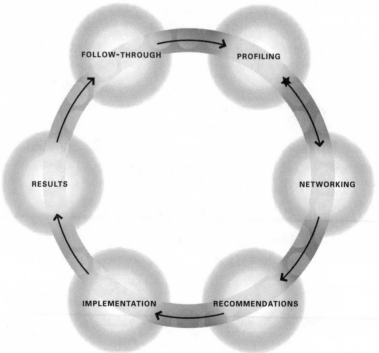

PROFILING THE CELEBRITY

Given the intricacies of advanced planning solutions, a thorough knowledge of the celebrity is required. This knowledge is the starting point of the Virtuous Cycle, because without it the desired results may be unattainable. There are thousands of profiling tools available to the professionals that work with a high-net-worth clientele. However, most of them are limited in their scope with a concentration on finances and assets. We have taken a more inclusive approach when profiling wealthy clients and find that our methodology not only delivers more balanced results but also enables us to uncover the personal priorities that may be influential in the planning effort.

Like the overall Virtuous Cycle, this phase has been checked against research data and tested by advisors. As a result, our profiling mechanism has a proven track record and has been adopted by countless high-end practitioners and leading financial and legal institutions. Broadly speaking, a client's profile is composed of the array of needs, desires, facts, figures, attitudes, perceptions, preferences, social dynamics, and thought processes that inform us about what can and should be done.

We have distilled the components of the client profile into seven interdependent sections, as follows, that collectively represent a client's complete state of affairs and better understand our clients. We refer to it as the Whole Client Model (Exhibit 9.2).

CLIENT

Understand the facts that will form the basis of the profile such as your age, gender, profession, income, net worth, and other relevant demographics.

GOALS

Understand your personal and professional goals and objectives, and your intentions for family and loved ones.

RELATIONSHIPS

Understand the relationships that are most important to you and those that carry some financial or emotional obligation.

FINANCIALS

Understand your current sources of income and any factors that may impact them in the short-or intermediate-term, as well as the structure, registration, and location of assets and liabilities.

ADVISORS

Know other advisors that you work with on a regular basis, including accountants, attorneys and business managers, and understand the role and influence each has in your life.

PROCESS

Understand your preferred method and frequency of interaction, and the level of detail you require.

INTERESTS

Understand those activities and topics that occupy your time and money, including hobbies, religion, politics, medicine, and philanthropy.

EXHIBIT 9.2: *The Whole Client Model*

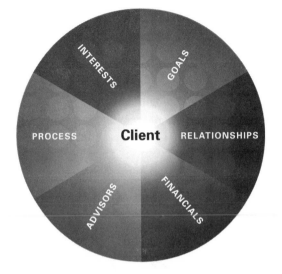

LEVERAGING A NETWORK OF EXPERTS

Socrates maintained that he was an ignorant man. He held this position despite his great knowledge or, more precisely, because of it; he knew enough to understand how much he did not know. High-quality advanced planners have a similar perspective in that they turn to niche experts to supplement their capabilities and create state-of-the-art solutions. Finding the right experts can be challenging since the best teammates are those that possess the right credentials, an effective working style, and high professional standards — a combination that is often hard to find and one that is highly desired. We have established the following criteria to filter and evaluate professionals:

SPECIFIC EXPERTISE. An advanced planning network is a group of professionals with complementary expertise. This means that each specialist plays a defined role in the process. We make sure to look for extensive training and experience in the specific discipline and check references and results.

INTEGRITY. High ethical standards are indispensable in all aspects of advanced planning and we require that every specialist in our network operate accordingly.

PROFESSIONALISM. Members of a network are an extension of the core advisor or advanced planner, and may work directly with clients or other organizations. Therefore, each expert must exude professionalism and reinforce it with the appropriate actions.

When a high-quality team of experts works together, it creates a multiplier effect, resulting in greater creativity and innovation on behalf of a wealthy client.

PRESENTING RECOMMENDATIONS

This phase is the junction of the Virtuous Cycle when our interpretation of a client's objectives is verified, our recommendations are assessed against those goals, and an agreement is reached regarding next steps.

First, the results of the Whole Client Model are reviewed with clients and their other advisors. It is imperative that everyone have the same understanding of the goals and issues at stake. If there is any meaningful disagreement – due to miscommunication, misinterpretation, changing circumstances or other factors – over the core premises and assumptions underlying the recommendations, the profiling phase must be revisited.

If the client profile is accurate and accepted, a discussion of possible strategies follows. If possible, more than one option should be presented along with the expected results and the advantages and disadvantages of each. This stage is most effective when the presentation is highly tailored to the client's situation and preferences.

Finally, a plan of action is identified. Sometimes a client can make an immediate decision to approve the plan and move forward. Sometimes a decision requires time for further evaluation or feedback from others. And, of course, there are times when a client doesn't feel the strategies are on target and will request minor tweaks, more significant alterations, or a complete overhaul. Ideally, the meeting should conclude with everyone in agreement about next steps.

IMPLEMENTATION

When a decision has been reached to pursue one or more advanced planning strategies, the implementation effort begins. Often, this is the most straightforward phase of the Virtuous Cycle because the barriers have been identified, solutions have been crafted, and a detailed plan is in place. This does not mean that implementation is easy; in most cases it calls for a tremendous amount of effort, persistence, and precision from everyone involved.

For instance, each step may consist of several underlying steps that add to the complexity and duration of the process. The actions required to obtain life insurance as part of an estate plan is a good example of the multifaceted nature of implementation. Even though all of the decisions have been made concerning the type, amount, and structure of the insurance, a number of steps remain. Finding the right product at the right price means skillful navigation of the underwriting process, which can be as varied as evaluating bids from multiple carriers, working directly with actuaries, or creating a fully customized product with a reinsurer. Depending on the circumstances, other steps to securing a policy, such as a physical assessment of the insured and premium funding must also be overseen.

However, implementation is a more mechanical process than an analytical one and familiar territory for the best advanced planners. As such, you can rely on the advanced planner to shepherd you through the process.

REVIEWING THE RESULTS

Results are what advanced planning is all about. Affluent clients want the results of the planning – tax savings, greater control, protection, and liquidity among them – not the effort itself, and expect to realize the benefits of the process. A review of results between advanced planners and clients can help punctuate the initiative and provides the forum to:

| Reiterate the client's goals and reconfirm the core profile.

| Identify any changes in status that may impact the effectiveness of the strategies.

| Evaluate the results against objectives and expectations.

| Ensure that the strategies are working as planned.

| Quantify the results in monetary terms.

| Discuss any environmental or regulatory changes that may impact the strategies.

| Outline next steps to address any changes or problems.

A review can be valuable for everyone involved and will also set the stage for the final phase of the Virtuous Cycle.

FOLLOW-THROUGH

Once advanced planning strategies are in place and delivering up to expectations, it is natural for all parties involved to turn their focus to more pressing matters. However, periodic involvement and continual assessments are needed to maintain a plan that accurately reflects your current situation and desires. In our experience, follow-through takes place in three key ways:

FOCUSED APPLICATIONS OF THE INNOVATION PROCESS. We develop and validate new strategies to address specific client problems on an ongoing basis. And often – due to changed regulations, evolved thinking, refined techniques, or different interpretations – a new strategy can deliver better results for an existing client. We regularly review our clientele to identify those individuals who may benefit from new strategies and products.

CELEBRITY-DRIVEN CONTACT. Any changes in circumstance – such as marriages and divorces, births and adoptions, illnesses and deaths, new deals, renegotiated or terminated contracts, and significant investments or acquisitions – can prompt celebrities or their advisors to reestablish contact with us. When this occurs, the celebrity's profile must be updated, the various phases of the Virtuous Cycle revisited, and the necessary changes implemented.

PERIODIC REVIEWS. Advanced planning is a subtle discipline in which very small changes can have an enormous impact. As a result, plans must be carefully monitored and maintained to continue working effectively. We regularly reach out to our wealthy clients to check the fit and effectiveness of each strategy and ensure that all components are working in concert.

IMPLICATIONS FOR CELEBRITIES AND THEIR ADVISORS

The Virtuous Cycle provides a systematic and tested guide to the advanced planning process. Adhering to its framework can help advanced planning specialists and celebrities have the most effective and productive interactions with an eye toward delivering the greatest results. Importantly, it should be viewed – and used – as a continuous process to capture and address meaningful changes in a timely fashion.

DRAWING *the Line*

There are numerous opportunities to bend or circumvent the law, including a number of well-known examples that should be avoided at all costs such as abusive trusts, phantom losses, and the inappropriate use of offshore structures and tax-shelters.

Too many wealthy individuals and their advisors are willing to take risks when they consider the potential benefits.

The complexity and ever-changing nature of tax codes throughout the world are a continual invitation for the unscrupulous to look for loop-holes and opportunities to reinterpret the law that may cross the line.

Most wealthy clients won't hesitate to bring legal action against their advisors if problems are encountered with specific strategies – and the most common defenses against liability are ignorance, transfer of responsibility, and pressure.

It requires extremely intelligent and proficient professionals to design these types of transactions and make them work. As a result, only highly principled and experienced advanced planners should be engaged to deal with significant wealth.

What might a celebrity

do to save US$20 million or more in income taxes? What might a celebrity do to keep his or her wealth from being lost because of a vindictive ex-spouse? What might a celebrity do to avoid having to reclaim an equity stake in a very profitable production company that's now in the hands of a disgruntled former employee?

In sharp contrast to the Virtuous Cycle – a process intended to deliver the most suitable and ethical advanced planning solutions for a wealthy client that fit squarely within the letter of the law – we often find that the opportunity to save taxes, decrease the size of legal settlements, and retain assets can drive even the most levelheaded people to questionable behavior.

Unfortunately, we have seen a number of successful celebrities under the guidance of their ethically impaired advisors take substantial risks to shield or grow their personal wealth even when the associated risks are unethical, inappropriate, or even illegal.

There is a great demand for services that enable taxes to be mitigated and for wealth to be enhanced, just as there are demands for services to shield assets from creditors and to tax-effectively facilitate the transference of ownership interests. And, there is little doubt that taking advantage of these services can be a smart course of action for any individual, provided the circumstances are right. But when these services are offered by a handful of unscrupulous or inexperienced advisors, celebrities can – and usually do – end up the losers.

Because advanced planning is a sophisticated and very specialized planning process that is unfamiliar to or misunderstood by many, it is easy for the uninitiated wealthy to find themselves on the wrong side of the legal line. In our experience, there are a broad variety of approaches that range from the legal to the questionable to the illegal. Below are some examples of abusive structures and strategies that should be avoided at all costs.

MISUSED TRUSTS

Abusive trust schemes usually entail the creation of a number of trusts, whether domestic or offshore, to which a wealthy individual assigns selected assets as well as income. The trusts are vertically layered so that each trust distributes income to the next trust. Bogus expenses are charged against the trust income, thereby reducing the taxable income. At the same time, the illusion of separation and control is created in order to shield the assets in the trust. Specifically, while the advisor is supposedly the trustee, the client actually controls the trust.

Quite a number of abusive trust arrangements exist. Often they are derivatives of legitimate planning techniques, but their promoters either claim tax benefits that will not withstand IRS scrutiny or administer them in such a way that even the legitimate benefits are forfeited. The following are some examples:

THE ABUSIVE ASSET MANAGEMENT COMPANY. An asset management company formed as a trust is created with the client appointed as the director. Meanwhile, the advisor is the trustee responsible for running the asset management company. The objective of this arrangement is for the client to convey the impression that he or she is not managing his or her businesses, thereby starting the layering process.

THE ABUSIVE BUSINESS TRUST. The client transfers a business to a trust, receiving certificates or units of beneficial interest. The business trust makes payments to the unit holders, the client or other trusts so that the business trust does not have to pay any taxes. The business trust can be set up so that the units are canceled at death or sold to the owner's heirs for a nominal cost, thus avoiding estate taxes.

THE ABUSIVE PRIVATE ANNUITY TRUST. The client sells appreciated property, typically real estate, to a trust in exchange for an annuity. The trust, which claims to have a full fair market value basis, sells the real estate and reinvests the money. The client claims he can recognize the built-in gain over the rest of his life, the trust is not a grantor trust and the trust is not included in his estate.

THE ABUSIVE FAMILY RESIDENCE TRUST. The client transfers his or her family residence (including furnishings) to a trust and receives units that are claimed to be part of a taxable exchange. The exchange results in a stepped-up basis for the property. At the same time, the owner does not report a gain. The trust is thus in the rental business and claims to rent the residence back to the owner. However, the owner and family pay no rent as they are identified as caretakers of the property.

THE ABUSIVE FINAL TRUST. When a number of abusive trusts are being employed, some clients create a final trust that holds the trust units of other abusive trusts and is the distributor of their income. Commonly, the final trust is created in a foreign jurisdiction, which imposes little if any tax on the trust.

Another misuse of trusts occurs when a wealthy individual employs offshore trusts solely as a way to attenuate tax liabilities. Too often we find that offshore trusts are over promoted as panaceas by people who do not fully understand the strict legal requirements that make these structures work for the affluent. Some of the more common complications include forced heirship rights, direct or indirect control, and inappropriate letters of wishes. While offshore trusts can be a very potent tool in an asset protection plan (see *Chapter 8: Asset Protection*), they are often wrongly used with promises that are impossible to keep.

PHANTOM LOSSES

Transactions that create phantom or imaginary losses also cross the line. Even though governments have made strides in cracking down on this type of transaction, a plethora of variations on this theme are still being discussed, explored, and used.

In these scenarios, a wealthy individual executes a paper transaction that theoretically results in a gain or a loss. On paper, the transaction has economic substance. In actuality it produces only a paper loss and, in practice, the transaction is a wash. The affluent individual then offsets other investment gains by this fraudulent one, or just deducts the loss from taxable income.

Often partnerships, corporate structures, and even special purpose entities are employed to shield wealthy individuals. Many times, leverage is used to magnify phantom losses. By using leverage, a wealthy individual can create a much larger phantom loss and also deduct the interest payments.

THE FINE LINE OF LEGALITY

Moving away from the black zone of clearly illegal acts, we will now enter the far more complicated and murky gray zone where the legality of a given strategy is open to interpretation. This is the dominion in which an advanced planner's integrity, or lack thereof, becomes readily apparent.

Given the many shades of gray, how does a celebrity know when a state-of-the-art strategy, especially a relatively new one, crosses the line of legality? When is aggressive too aggressive?

A strategy is too aggressive, for example, if its sole economic benefit is to enable a celebrity to illegally pay less in taxes or dodge legitimate creditors. In the former case, the advisor is engaged in tax laundering for his or her wealthy clients; in the latter, the advisor is hiding money and is usually involved in fraudulent conveyances.

During our interactions with other advisors and celebrities, we have seen many strategies that are aggressive to the point of being highly questionable. Because so many of these strategies require complete customization, it is nearly impossible to have a standard definition and each instance must be evaluated separately and on its own merits. Nevertheless, when the celebrity engages in a series of transactions whose sole objective is to mitigate income taxes, for example, caution is well advised.

It's incumbent on all professionals, however, not to employ strategies that are devised for the express purpose of evading taxes or secluding money and, above all, not to employ strategies that may ever compromise their clients. Ideally, advanced planning strategies are conceived and evaluated in the context of a comprehensive financial plan. At a minimum, they must be both rational and justifiable. If a client insists on employing strategies that are too aggressive or highly questionable, even after the legal and ethical issues and the pitfalls have been pointed out, a conscientious advisor should end the relationship.

WHY WALK THE FINE LINE?

So why do some advisors and their clients knowingly go over the line? Why do they take risks that carry potentially severe consequences? What is the primary justification for being overaggressive?

To address this issue, we examined 118 tax cases. Each one can be characterized as not being, *prima facie*, illegal. We are not talking about money laundering, for example, but rather cases in which the strategies employed were highly aggressive and upon close evaluation proved to have crossed the line. The penalties for the affluent clients involved included fines, interest, paying back taxes and, in several of the cases, the loss of significant assets as the questionable strategies were voided by the courts.

For the advisors, there were also severe penalties. Some lost their professional licenses, while an astonishing 109 out of the 118 were sued by their affluent clients (Exhibit 10.1), a percentage that should deter any thoughts of crossing the line for either party.

EXHIBIT 10.1: *Percent of Affluent Clients Who Sued Their Advisors*

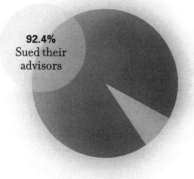

92.4%
Sued their
advisors

N=118 cases

By coding legal documents and employing a cluster analytic methodology, we are able to categorize the primary justification for being overaggressive into three categories that also show the meaningful differences between the motivations of the affluent clients and their advisors (Exhibit 10.2).

EXHIBIT 10.2: *Primary Justification*

JUSTIFICATION	AFFLUENT CLIENTS	THEIR ADVISORS
Ignorance	5.6%	28.8%
Transfer of Responsibility	79.8%	11.9%
Pressure	14.6%	59.3%
N = 118 Cases		

IGNORANCE *(a.k.a., the "I didn't know" defense).* In this case, affluent clients claimed to have been unaware of what was going on and ignorant of the consequences of their actions. Interestingly, they did not blame their advisors for leading them astray. At the same time, more than a quarter of the advisors also excused their behavior by claiming ignorance. If they were truly ignorant, this demonstrates that far too many self-proclaimed experts in this field are in over their heads, and when they came across an enticing strategy, they failed—or elected not—to educate themselves on the possible ramifications and consequences.

TRANSFER OF RESPONSIBILITY *(a.k.a., the "It was his idea" defense).* Wealthy clients turn to advisors because they want to benefit from their expertise, but when it comes to wealth maximization, those clients are often unable to fully understand and evaluate the recommendations they receive. So it's easy to pass the buck and blame their advisors when things go wrong. This was far and away the most common justification adopted by affluent clients, and it's also the reasoning behind their lawsuits. Advisors looking to dodge responsibility will in turn sometimes blame other advisors, and, in at least one case we know of, accused their own client of having led them astray.

PRESSURE *(a.k.a., the "I was forced to do it" defense).* Some clients claimed that they were compelled to go wrong because of the promise of financial benefits and their financial needs. For advisors, financial and competitive pressures were the leading justification for their actions. In order to win business, the advisors concluded that they had to be able to provide services that differentiated them and, unfortunately, they sometimes went too far.

THE HIDDEN JUSTIFICATION

The above justifications, based on an analysis of various documents, identify the legal rationales for why some advisors and clients are overaggressive. However, based on our work in the field, we have found a hidden justification for being overaggressive that correlates with both the transfer of responsibility and the high pressure scenarios: the cost-versus-benefit calculation. In other words, given the amount of money involved, the risk of being caught is deemed worth taking.

Playing the audit lottery, for example, is very attractive to a number of the wealthy. The amount of time, energy and mental firepower that the government can bring to bear is rarely equal to the clever ways that some advisors can alter and hide assets through a dizzying series of ingenious transactions. As a result, a select portion of wealthy individuals and their advisors will continue to be overaggressive because they perceive the benefits to outweigh the risks.

Factor in the justifications put forth by the affluent and their advisors in their defense, and the fact that so many advisors are operating beyond their level of proficiency (see *Chapter 11: Finding the Right Professional*), and it becomes evident that we'll continue to see the use of strategies that will cause problems down the road.

A PERSONAL NOTE

It's up to advanced planning specialists, through their understanding of the legal consequences and their ethical grounding, to draw a clear line that governs their actions. Pushing the envelope can be enticing and, for many advisors, a challenging and intriguing process of sophisticated puzzle solving. But we feel there is an absolute need to view all strategies through an ethical lens.

With sad regularity, celebrities come to us to implement strategies they have heard about that, upon closer examination, are over the line. As noted, there are such a wide variety of advanced planning strategies celebrities can use to legitimately transfer, protect, and enhance their wealth that we feel crossing the line – with all the potential financial and personal downsides – is just foolish.

IMPLICATIONS FOR CELEBRITIES AND THEIR ADVISORS

The benefits of advanced planning are clearly top priorities for wealthy celebrities. Given the amount of money involved, and the motivation of celebrities and their advisors to preserve and grow that wealth, new strategies are constantly being devised (see *Chapter 5: Advanced Planning*). Some of these strategies are perfectly legal, but others may not be, and should be inspected closely before any action is taken. Celebrities, their advisors, and the advanced planning specialist should be clear about their goals, their limitations, and their ethical parameters with one another upfront, so there are no surprises along the way.

High-quality advanced planners will scour the universe for emerging strategies. And while the use of such strategies can be enticing, the financial benefits should not lure celebrities or advanced planners into crossing ethical or legal boundaries. Moreover, it's the advanced planner's responsibility to draw the line at the edge of innovation rather than take a risk, however measured, that could jeopardize a client's wealth and reputation.

11

FINDING THE
Right Professional

AT A GLANCE

Most legal and financial professionals do not have sufficient knowledge and experience with advanced planning to warrant serving celebrity clients in this capacity.

It is important that celebrities and their advisors know what they need from an advanced planner and to screen diligently so as to avoid scams, ill-conceived plans, and legal hassles.

There are five qualities that should be present in all qualified advanced planners: integrity, technical expertise, a network of niche specialists, a focus on client needs, and experience with other wealthy celebrities.

Managing the relationship with an advanced planner can also deliver better results for everyone involved, and can be accomplished with minimal but firm oversight from the celebrity and his or her outside advisors.

Advanced planning, as we practice it, is not the fare of most financial and legal advisors. In fact, it's the exact opposite. Relatively speaking, there are few high-quality advanced planning specialists and even fewer that are attuned to the world of celebrity wealth.

Finding and working with a top-notch advanced planner can be a thorny undertaking, further complicated by the fact that the specialist must be aware of cutting-edge strategies, be able to leverage a network of niche experts when appropriate, and work effectively with their celebrity client through the Virtuous Cycle.

Unanticipated misfortunes and the exigencies of a generally litigious environment aside, many celebrities often need the services of advanced planners as part of their broad financial plan as a means of significantly preserving and growing their wealth. Moreover, celebrities and their advisors must work with advanced planners to find tailored solutions rather than agreeing to proceed with generic strategies.

Clearly, when it comes to choosing from the array of practitioners who characterize themselves as advanced planners, it pays to be skeptical. Any wealthy individual, but especially a wealthy celebrity, needs to select a specialist carefully and, to that end, this chapter will focus on how to choose such advanced planning specialists and how to get the most from the relationship.

FINDING A HIGH-QUALITY ADVANCED PLANNER

There are a multitude of ways the wealthy and successful locate the range of professionals with whom they do business, but the most common and reliable method is a referral from a trusted source. The same logic holds true for advanced planners. The nature of all high-end, specialized services makes referrals an important risk-mitigation step when selecting a provider, as demonstrated below:

INTANGIBLE SERVICES. For most celebrities, advanced planning is something of a mystery. The strategies cannot be seen or touched or evaluated directly. Thus, it's wise for celebrities to turn to people whose judgment they trust for guidance.

COMPLEX PROCESSES. In our experience, the financial concerns of celebrities are unique and complicated. A celebrity seeking a professional to deal with the intricacies of his or her world should ask specifically for referrals to specialists with proven track records in their discipline.

THE NEED FOR AUTHORITIES. We have yet to meet a celebrity – actually any affluent person – who did not want to work with an expert, a true authority on developing and implementing legal and financial strategies for the wealthy. Any individual that does not possess the aptitude to rate a professional's credentials, should turn to other celebrities or, better yet, other authorities, for their opinions.

Nearly all of our clients come to us through referrals — from existing clients or other professionals — and this is the norm for all advanced planners catering to any segment of the financial elite.

While celebrities may introduce their peers and other advisors will bring in advanced planning specialists they've vetted, the client must still control the selection process. To help in this process, there are a number of guidelines to consider when selecting an advanced planner.

FIVE CRITERIA FOR SELECTING AN ADVANCED PLANNER

The competencies of any legal or financial professional are often difficult to effectively judge. This is even more so with the field of advanced planning, as the quality of some of the strategies provided can't be truly evaluated until it's too late — if at all.

An asset protection plan, for instance, can be determined to work only if you are in the unfortunate position of being taken to court. And if the advanced planner did a less than competent job, it will then be too late to correct the situation. Or consider a state-of-the-art estate plan. Will it work as promised? You will never know; only your heirs will.

This often means that celebrities will have to trust the judgment of the advanced planner and the judgment of their other advisors. This does not, however, mean you can completely remove yourself from the process or hire a specialist without properly vetting the professional. On the contrary, it is ultimately the client's responsibility to ensure that due diligence is conducted on any prospective advanced planner. At the end of the day, you must trust your advisors, but first those advisors must earn that trust.

We have found that there are five criteria that prove to be highly useful when selecting an advanced planner. They are:

CRITERION #1 **Proven integrity.**

CRITERION #2 **Extensive technical expertise.**

CRITERION #3 **Access to niche experts.**

CRITERION #4 **Sensitivity to client needs.**

CRITERION #5 **Experience in working with affluent celebrities.**

Advanced planning specialists regularly deal with sophisticated, legal-based strategies and complex financial products. By carefully using these criteria to screen prospective advanced planners, it is possible to avoid the plethora of financial and legal advisors who target celebrities and are more than happy to provide much less than they promise or charge for.

CRITERION #1 **Proven integrity.**

Integrity is first on the list of criteria, and for good reason. The veracity of your advanced planning specialist is a critical and intrinsic part of safeguarding your wealth.

While not restricted to advanced planning, the attorneys in our survey estimated that about two in five of their top celebrity clients reported having been cheated at one time or another by a corrupt advisor (Exhibit 11.1). These celebrities mistakenly took the advice of these advisors, only recognizing the scam when it was too late. The result can, more often than not, be a very expensive lesson in life.

EXHIBIT 11.1: *Cheated by Corrupt Advisors*

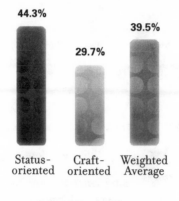

44.3%

39.5%

29.7%

Status-   Craft-   Weighted
oriented   oriented   Average

N=1,015 celebrities
(based on 203 entertainment attorneys)

Many attorneys and their celebrity clients have been approached with misleading asset protection solutions such as "unbreakable secret trusts" and "your own bank" to the marketing of pure trusts otherwise known as patriot trusts, contract trusts, final trusts, foreign common law trust organizations, and complex trust systems. About half of celebrities have been pitched asset protection scams (Exhibit 11.2) so it's important to be able to distinguish between the experts and the posers, and separate the bright line strategies from those that cross the line.

EXHIBIT 11.2: *Were Pitched Asset Protection Scams*

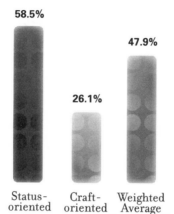

58.5%

47.9%

26.1%

Status-
oriented

Craft-
oriented

Weighted
Average

N=1,015 celebrities
(based on 203 entertainment attorneys)

The nature of fame means wealthy celebrities can be a prime target for corrupt advisors and opportunists. This in turns means extra care must be taken when evaluating a new provider and before entering into a working relationship. We often use the following questions to help assess an individual's *modus operandi:*

> **Ask the advanced planner under what conditions he or she would fire a client.** As previously noted, sometimes we are asked by clients to help them implement an illegal or questionable strategy. In all cases we will research the law and explain the breach, and explore other ways of achieving the goal and recommend approaches that fit our operating model. If celebs and their outside advisors insist on their initial requests, we will no longer do business with them.

> **Ask the advanced planning specialist what he or she would not do.** In effect, you are determining where the advanced planner has drawn the line that defines his or her acceptable range of behavior. How far into the gray area is the advanced

planner willing to travel? Aggressive and innovative strategies are good; ones that stray into questionable territory can have lasting, and negative, repercussions for everyone involved.

CRITERION #2 Extensive technical expertise.

Everyone wants to work with a professional that brings talent and capabilities to the equation. In addition to the scammers we referenced earlier, we find that many well-intentioned professionals lack the expertise that is needed to do the job.

In a study sponsored by *Trusts & Estates* magazine, we found that only a small percentage of private client lawyers who identified themselves as asset protection experts were indeed knowledgeable about many of the strategies with which the wealthy can legitimately protect their wealth. Additionally, there was a significant gap between their current competency levels and their ideal skill levels. Even though most readily positioned themselves as asset protection experts, just 16 percent of the lawyers surveyed rated themselves as authorities on asset protection (Exhibit 11.3).

Another example of lacking skills is the number of private client lawyers, just 13 percent, who were very familiar with the Uniform Fraudulent Transfer Act. Importantly, the attorneys themselves agreed that there was a competence gap and, overall, about three-quarters agreed that they needed to become more knowledgeable about asset protection strategies.

EXHIBIT 11.3: *Delivering Asset Protection Expertise*

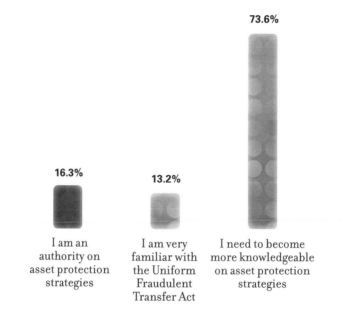

N=227 Self-identified asset protection lawyers

Another indication that many private client lawyers need to enhance their asset protection expertise is the meaningful number who are unfamiliar with some of the more common strategies in the field (Exhibit 11.4). While most were comfortable with mainstream techniques such as corporate structures, outright gifts to family members, and limited liability companies, far fewer claimed knowledge in areas such as offshore self-settled trusts, life insurance, and equity stripping.

EXHIBIT 11.4: *Familiar with Specific Asset Protection Strategies*

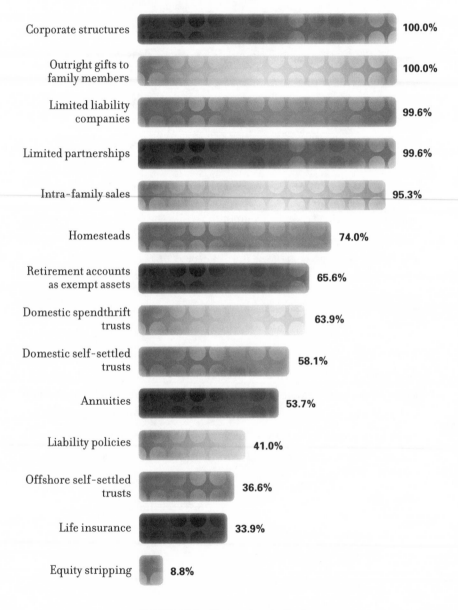

Corporate structures	100.0%
Outright gifts to family members	100.0%
Limited liability companies	99.6%
Limited partnerships	99.6%
Intra-family sales	95.3%
Homesteads	74.0%
Retirement accounts as exempt assets	65.6%
Domestic spendthrift trusts	63.9%
Domestic self-settled trusts	58.1%
Annuities	53.7%
Liability policies	41.0%
Offshore self-settled trusts	36.6%
Life insurance	33.9%
Equity stripping	8.8%

N=227 Self-identified asset protection lawyers

In short, this survey revealed that most private client lawyers were not adequately prepared to offer asset protection planning at the level needed for significant wealth. Thus there are a number of factors to consider when appraising a professional's technical expertise, including:

| The history and experience of the referral source;

| Educational background;

| Professional experience;

| Professional licenses and designations;

| Association with industry organizations;

| Publications and speaking engagements; and

| Recognition from peers in the financial and legal industries.

It is your wealth at risk. Consequently, while the input of others can be valuable, it's your obligation to make sure that the chosen advanced planning specialist passes muster.

CRITERION #3 **Access to niche experts.**

As discussed in *Chapter 9: The Virtuous Cycle*, providing the type of expertise needed very often requires a team of leading-edge experts. No matter how technically adept an advanced planner is, he or she can't know all the nuances about every strategy that can be used to protect and enhance wealth. No one is an advanced planning polymath. Rather, they must have access to an array of high-quality niche experts who can work hand-in-hand with them and their wealthy clients.

It's wise to have a discussion with the advanced planner about his or her network of experts. Some of the questions you should ask are:

| Who are they?

| Why did you choose them?

| What is their area of expertise?

| How does everyone work together?

| How are these experts compensated?

Not only does this approach enable you to better gauge the capabilities of an advanced planner, but it may also provide some insight into the way the advanced planning specialist works. Very likely, you and your other advisors will be interacting with these niche experts, so you should understand their roles.

CRITERION #4   Sensitivity to client needs.

It's not a client's job to identify or explain strategies to an advanced planner; rather it's up to the specialist to understand each client's goals and bring innovative ideas, concepts, and methodologies to the table. It is important to find a professional who will spend the time needed to learn as much as possible about your financial situation, your objectives, the issues and peculiarities that must be considered, your doubts and concerns, and your personal preferences. Only then will it be possible to identify the opportunities and the best way to realize them.

Keeping the focus on the client is one way to ensure that recommendations are suitable, goals are met, and interactions are efficient and effective. This is why the Virtuous Cycle is central to wealth maximization and why the Whole Client Model plays a critical role in the conceptualization of plans (see *Chapter 9: The Virtuous Cycle*).

CRITERION #5   Experience in working with affluent celebrities.

Celebrities are a distinct type of client. Their backgrounds and personal experiences, the lifestyle and business environment, and the perks and stresses of the profession all add up to a very unique situation (see *Part I: Spotlight on Celebrities*). While they may have similar levels of wealth, they are very different from the owners of manufacturing companies, Fortune 500 executives, heirs to significant fortunes or hedge fund managers, for instance.

While advanced planning is applicable to all manner of the wealthy, the world of fame and fortune provides idiosyncrasies that can't be overlooked or underestimated. It is, therefore, valuable to find and engage an advanced planner who is attuned to your profession. Research and education is mandatory, but it is the experience working with celebrity clients that provides the most useful and practical insights. And the more similarities there are among a client base, the more readily an advanced planner can spot issues and opportunities, and adapt and deploy strategies.

HOW TO WORK WITH AN ADVANCED PLANNER

Finding a top-notch advanced planner is not enough — the relationship must be managed to get the most out of it. The process can be an education of sorts; in the end, celebrities shouldn't expect to be proficient in the field but they should have a clear sense of what they are paying for and what actions will be taken. Therefore, it's very important to understand how the advanced planner works and the rationale behind the recommendations that are made.

The following three guidelines can help in this regard:

GUIDELINE #1 **Ask for an explanation of the Virtuous Cycle.**

GUIDELINE #2 **Ask about alternative ways to achieve your agenda.**

GUIDELINE #3 **Ask how the various strategies will interact.**

GUIDELINE #1 **Explanation of the Virtuous Cycle**

Most advanced planners will have their own variation on the Virtuous Cycle, but the steps we detailed are key to the process and cannot be compromised. By asking them to discuss their philosophical and operational approach, you will know what to expect from your advanced planning specialist and what stages will call for personal involvement.

GUIDELINE #2 Alternative Ways to Achieve Your Agenda

It is a rare situation or circumstance that has a solitary solution. In most cases, there are many possible methods that can result in similar outcomes. It's essential to understand the trade-offs associated with the various options before making a decision. You, in conjunction with the advanced planning specialist and your other advisors, need to spend the time reviewing the possibilities in order to find the strategy that will best meet your needs.

GUIDELINE #3 How the Various Strategies Interact

The goal of advanced planning is wealth preservation and enhancement. This means that any advanced planning strategies must take into consideration your broad financial plans and objectives to be effective. It also means that many elements are often designed to work together to create synergies. At the same time, the wrong combination of strategies can undermine all the preceding efforts. Avoiding this outcome often requires full disclosure and a collaborative working relationship between all the advisors – championed by you.

A PERSONAL NOTE

We regularly meet with affluent clients and their other advisors who want to relinquish total responsibility for this component of their financial wellbeing. We have found that working *with* clients is far more effective than blindly working *for* them. Having a motivated, engaged, and informed client will result in the best decisions and the best results.

IMPLICATIONS FOR CELEBRITIES AND THEIR ADVISORS

Getting the most from advanced planning requires the assistance and involvement of a high-quality specialist. As such, the most important decision celebs can make is who to work with toward the preservation and enhancement of their wealth, seeking honest and trustworthy professionals at the cutting edge of their profession. Leveraging peer and advisory relationships for referrals to experts can be a great start. Celebrity clients must also be committed to the process, carefully screening prospective providers against established criteria to ensure technical aptitude, and actively managing the relationship. This doesn't mean full-time involvement; other advisors can take part in this process, acting as a proxy for their clients and shouldering some of the burden to get things done.

AFTERWORD:
The Celebrity Family Office

As more celebrities join the ranks of the affluent and many of today's wealthy celebrities transition to the universe of the ultra-affluent, there will be greater demand for the products and services that allow them to do more than just manage their wealth — the focus will be on maximizing their wealth. Fortunately, the mercurial financial and legal environment creates numerous opportunities for celebrities to both protect and magnify wealth using advanced planning strategies. We, of course, know from experience that helping celebrities maximize their wealth can be a lengthy, involved, and complicated process that must take into consideration the many aspects of celebrityhood that are not be relevant for other wealthy individuals.

One of the ways we have accomplished this is through the creation of a celebrity family office — the new business paradigm for wealthy, successful celebrities. Family offices, as a rule, are a way to aggregate and centralize the many facets of wealth management. The driving rationale of every family office is that the collective assets of a family are more efficaciously managed by a single specialty organization dedicated to, and capable of, catering to the group needs and wants of an exceptionally wealthy family (and, when appropriate, the needs and wants of individual family members).

Conceptually, the family office is the last word in providing financial coordination and management with a solid and sometimes near exclusive focus on the investments of the family. When a more holistic approach is taken, as is increasingly the case, an affluent family benefits from a broader platform of capabilities that may include tax-related and administrative services, advanced planning, and a portfolio of lifestyle services that create synergies and can maximize assets in accord with a family's financial, philanthropic, and personal agenda.

We anticipate more wealthy celebrities will be exploring the benefits of family offices – whether it's through a conventional entity dedicated to a single family, in partnership with other families in a multifamily office structure, or through a respected institution that specializes in serving the ultra-affluent.

The celebrity family office is a unique advisory organization that combines the best aspects of traditional business management and classic family offices with a range of highly specialized capabilities. Ultimately, the celebrity family office will be the preferred way for affluent celebrities to ensure customization in the oversight and management of their finances, access the range of ancillary services that support their lifestyles, retain privacy and control over their fortunes, and fully maximize their wealth.

APPENDICES

APPENDIX A: research METHODOLOGY

In studying the wealthy – any segment of the wealthy – we don't engage in probability sampling. Instead, we employ a nonprobability sampling process commonly referred to as snowball sampling. The difference between nonprobability and probability sampling is that the former does not involve random selection while the latter does. This does not mean that nonprobability samples are not representative of the population; it does mean that nonprobability samples cannot depend upon the rationale of probability theory.

However, this approach is not viable when it comes to surveying affluent celebrities. For reasons of privacy and access, the ability to construct a workable sample set of wealthy celebrities is nearly impossible. Consequently, we utilized an unobtrusive empirical approach to collecting quantitative data on this hard-to-access, low-incidence sample.

We employed an accepted approach in the social sciences known as an intermediary-based judgment sampling methodology. That is, we turned to entertainment attorneys as our surrogate for the celebrities themselves. The attorneys responded to the survey questions using empirical and experiential data on five of their celebrity clients. Both the attorneys and the celebrities had to meet specific criteria in order to be included in the research study (see *Chapter 1: The Lens of Celebrity Wealth*).

Intermediary-based judgment sampling is essential for situations in which a targeted sample cannot be otherwise reached and where the selected intermediaries play a critical role. Precautions were taken to minimize or eliminate the intrinsic risks of this approach: the accuracy of the intermediary's perception and the relevance of these findings to the entire universe of affluent celebrities. Until other viable methods of conducting empirical investigations are identified, this methodology is the most effective and meaningful way to quantitatively understand unique sub-segments of private wealth.

APPENDIX B: safe and SOUND

WITH KIND ASSISTANCE FROM MITCH GITTER, DEFENDER SECURITY, INC.

As discussed in *Chapter 2: Both Sides of Fame*, celebrities can often attract the less savory elements of society – in other words, criminals. Without question, the top priority of most celebrities is the safety of their loved ones and themselves. These concerns prompt many of them to take precautionary steps. This section includes the common approaches taken by private security professionals to help wealthy individuals and families protect human and capital assets.

CRISIS CONTINGENCY PLANNING. Clients and selected loved ones are provided with training on how to manage a crisis situation. The training focuses on reducing the likelihood of such situations and how to minimize risk should such a situation occur. Training is often based on simulation exercises, including intense role-playing scenarios, and small group discussion sessions.

SELF-DEFENSE. In a related vein, there is a recent trend among the wealthy to assume more responsibility for their own protection. Schools and training facilities that previously worked exclusively with protection specialists are increasingly finding executives and wealthy individuals in their classrooms, at their firing ranges, and enrolled in their defensive driving courses. The goal for most clients is to disable an attacker long enough to escape or for help to arrive.

CLOSE PROTECTION PERSONNEL. Most celebrities are familiar with bodyguards and some have certainly had one or more on their payroll at some point. Increasingly, we hear about wealthy individuals including celebrities asking for a more advanced and comprehensive form of defensive support. Often this requires personnel that can blend in with the client and his or her entourage, indiscernible to any source of threat. It also includes extensive advance work and reconnaissance, examining vehicles and buildings that clients and their loved ones will use, preparing emergency evacuation routes, and liaising with police and security organizations, when appropriate.

TRANSPORTER SERVICES. This is a variation of close protection that is used when clients and their loved ones are moving between locations and require chaperones. The use of transporter services, like all other aspects of personal security for the affluent, is on the rise. Until recently, many types of transporter services were used primarily for property (see below); today specially trained chauffeurs in vehicles equipped with contact tasers and tear gas grenades, backed by on-call retrieval teams, are becoming the norm.

BACKGROUND INVESTIGATIONS. All too often, the weak link in a celebrity's personal and professional life is people on the inside. Everyone with access to clients, their loved ones, their finances, and their business interests should be thoroughly investigated. Moreover, such scrutiny should occur periodically and without notice to ensure the ongoing security of the family.

IDENTITY PROTECTION. Identity theft is the fastest-growing crime in the country. While it's a hit-and-run crime, the hit can be painful to wealthy individuals. We regularly find that many people don't adhere to the same level of precaution to protect their confidential information at home and in work environments. Education can go a long way toward mitigating identity theft, and continuously tracking the use of client identities can provide additional insurance.

COUNTER-SURVEILLANCE SERVICES. Protecting the details of important and private personal and business interactions can be assured by regularly sweeping rooms and communications equipment, such as phones and computers, for surveillance equipment. Many of our affluent clients find that negotiations between two parties with conflicting agendas – divorces, contract terms, business transfers, and deal and project development – can benefit from the use of counter-surveillance services.

HIGH-TECH SECURITY SYSTEMS. When it comes to residential security, options range from very basic to extremely sophisticated. Some state-of-the-art systems include outer perimeter detection that informs the homeowner if there is unauthorized movement on the property, intrusion detection for the exterior of the house, and an alarm system in the house that features motion sensors, closed circuit cameras, laser grids, and pressure-sensitive switches attached to the artwork. In some home systems, activating the alarms can detain intruders until the police arrive, employing such features such as automatically deployed, locking steel curtains.

SAFE ROOMS. Safe rooms – sometimes known as panic rooms – are becoming a standard part of many buildings, especially those that may attract thieves and interlopers. A safe room can provide short-term protection for the occupants of a home, yacht or office while they wait for help to arrive and allow for direct communication with law enforcement and security professionals.

A high-quality safe room should include cameras and monitors displaying the entrance to the room and other areas of the building, special ventilation that protects those inside from chemical and biological agents, and multiple ways to communicate with the outside world that cannot be easily disconnected or compromised, along with gas masks, bottled water and nonperishable food.

Increasingly, safe rooms are being constructed to function as command centers from which the alarms and weapons – such as non-lethal shotguns and tear gas – protecting the building can be controlled remotely.

PROTECTING COLLECTIBLES. There are two scenarios with collectibles that require precautions: when the collection is in residence and when it's in motion. Home security systems are generally designed to protect any collectibles in the structure and, often, special measures are taken with exceptionally valuable items. Other collectibles, such as fine art, may be outside the home for a variety of reasons. When art is in motion – during delivery, moving between homes, professional restoration, traveling exhibitions, on temporary loan to charities or museums, for instance – it requires planning and coordination. This may include the use of specialty transport firms and background investigations on the assigned professionals, radio frequency chips that can track the location of specific items, and specialty insurance.

THE BOTTOM LINE

Many of the situations that would require the services described above are highly improbable, but ultra-wealthy individuals have the luxury of using just a sliver of their wealth to enhance the odds of avoiding such security problems and creating a stronger and more extensive zone of protection around themselves and the people and things they hold dear. It is a small price to pay for the peace-of-mind that comes from knowing you did everything within your power to be as safe and secure as possible.

MITCH GITTER, President of Defender Security Services, Inc., is a leading authority on crisis management and personal security solutions for the wealthy including celebrities, hedge fund managers, family offices and affluent business owners.
www.defendersecurityinc.com • mgitter@defendersecurityinc.com

About the Authors

RUSS ALAN PRINCE is the world's leading authority on private wealth, the author of 40 books on the topic, and a highly-sought counselor to individuals and families with significant global resources, and their advisors.
www.russalanprince.com • russ@russalanprince.com

HANNAH SHAW GROVE is a widely recognized author, columnist, coach, consultant, and speaker, and an expert on the mindset, behaviors, concerns, preferences, and finances of high-net-worth individuals.
www.hsgrove.com • hannah@hsgrove.com

RICHARD J. FLYNN is a principal of the accounting and business management firm Rothstein Kass, head of the Family Office Group, and an advanced planning specialist.
www.rkco.com • rflynn@rkco.com

About the Publisher

THE PRIVATE JET LIFESTYLE MAGAZINE

Elite Traveler is the world's leading luxury lifestyle publication. With BPA-audited distribution aboard private jets, mega-yachts and other high-end venues in over 90 countries, it is designed specifically for a super-affluent, global readership that includes owners of significant businesses, C-Level executives at multi-nationals, athletes, entertainers, royalty, government leaders and their families.

For its over 575,000 readers every issue, *Elite Traveler's* unique editorial is specifically targeted to the private jet lifestyle, and delivers detailed coverage in key categories such as watches, jewelry, fashion, automotive, real estate and travel. *Elite Traveler* is an indispensable personal assistant for the ultra-wealthy in their quest for the best in supreme luxury products and services.

Elite Traveler is part of Universal Media, a global communications and publishing firm. More information is available at www.elite-traveler.com.